SAVING BABYLON
The Heart of an Army Interrogator in Iraq

"A gripping, highly readable and surprising book. . . . An inspiring volume, sure to become a classic."
—Joe Bauman, *Deseret News*

"Paul Holton provides an intensely personal account of war and its aftermath, something you'll never get from the legions of war correspondents who tried, and mostly failed, to cover this war."
—Glenn Reynolds, InstaPundit.com

"COMPELLING . . . FASCINATING . . . *Saving Babylon* is a well-written story of a soldier's extraordinary experiences during the Iraq War. A must read for every American interested in the *truth* about the liberation of Iraq."
—Joe Weber, *New York Times* best-selling author

President George W. Bush commended Paul Holton at the National Prayer Breakfast:

"Our people in uniform understand the high calling they have answered because they see the nation and the lives they are changing. A guardsman from Utah named Paul Holton has described seeing an Iraqi girl crying and decided then and there to help that child and others like her. By enlisting aid through the Internet, Chief Warrant Officer Holton had arranged the shipment of more than 1,600 aid packages from overseas. . . . Our work in a troubled part of the world goes on, and what we have begun, we will finish."

SAVING BABYLON

SAVING BABYLON

The Heart of
an Army Interrogator in Iraq

PAUL HOLTON

PERIHELION PRESS

Published by Perihelion Press, 3641 Little Rock Drive, Provo, UT 84604
www.perihelionpress.com

Cover design by Diane McIntosh, K.C. Muscolino
Interior design by Marny K. Parkin, K.C. Muscolino

Cover photo by Spc. Sean Kimmons, courtesy of U.S. Army.

Holton, Paul Roy
Saving Babylon : the heart of an army interrogator in Iraq

Library of Congress Control Number: 2005925715

ISBN 978-1-933434-00-1

*To the Iraqi people who believed in freedom
and the American soldiers who were willing to fight for it.*

Contents

Military Terminology and Acronyms

AK-47 (Kalashnikov) Soviet-made assault rifle

APO Army Post Office

BIAP Baghdad International Airport

C-130 (Hercules) Primary aircraft for troop transport and for para-dropping troops and equipment

CID Criminal Investigation Division

CPA Coalition Provisional Authority

CW Chief Warrant Officer

IED improvised explosive device

JAG Judge Advocate General

JIF Joint Interrogation Facility

JOC Joint Operations Center

M16 Semi-automatic rifle carried by U.S. troops

MET Mobile Exploitation Team

MI Military Intelligence

MIT	Mobile Interrogation Team
MOPP	Mission Oriented Protective Posture (nuclear, biological and chemical protection worn by soldiers; MOPP-4 being the highest level)
MP	Military Police
MP5	Submachine gun used primarily by Special Operations units
MRE	meal, ready to eat
MWR	morale, welfare, and recreation
POW	prisoner of war
PX	Post Exchange
R&R	rest and recuperation
Scud	The NATO reporting name for a short-range Soviet surface-to-surface ballistic missile (not an acronym)
SRP	Soldier Readiness Process
TOC	Tactical Operations Center
WMD	Weapon of Mass Destruction

Iraq

Acknowledgements

Saving Babylon represents the culmination of a series of miraculous events and the efforts of dozens of devoted individuals. My gratitude seems small in comparison to their contributions.

My military assignments have had a significant impact on my family. My sweet wife, Keeyeon, has kept the faith during my many months of deployment. My daughter, Dana, and my three sons, Daniel, Michael, and Matthew, have sacrificed much in supporting me in my military endeavors. Special hugs for my granddaughter, Katella. National Guard is more than just a "weekend a month"—it's a way of life that has sent me on dangerous assignments and to distant war zones. In addition to my gratitude, my family will always have my love.

Every day I spent in Iraq I was surrounded by like-minded folks from my Utah National Guard unit. They showed compassion, dedication, and patriotism in every task. When they salute the flag, you can feel their love for America.

My closest military buddies, Major Price, Chief Allen, and Specialist Heimdal, kept me on track and helped me focus my efforts. They supported me in both my military assignments and making a difference for many Iraqi children. They showed me over and over what kindhearted people can do—especially when they work together.

Innumerable Iraqis and American civilians put everything on the line to forward the cause of freedom. Among them were many faithful friends, including my interpreter, Renda, who seamlessly flowed between Arabic and English, making much of my work possible.

Hundreds of pages of detailed journal entries, notes, and interviews benefited from the inspired work of my editors, Greg and Elain Witt, to become a readable record of my Iraq experience.

Scott Evensen, good friend and computer guru, has been the glue that held all of my efforts together. He turned my emails into a blog, enabling thousands of people to check in daily to see what Chief Wiggles had to say.

And to my Father in Heaven, gratitude for leading me to children in need and then bringing me home safely to tell the story.

Introduction

When I joined the Army National Guard as an 18-year-old scared kid in the 1960s, I hoped my enlistment might spare me from going to Vietnam. It did.

Who would have guessed that six years later I'd re-enlist, but I did. Patriotic passion was pumping in my veins; a sense of military mission had seeped into my pores.

I started out as a boy unsure of my duty, but grew into man driven by duty. Duty to God. Duty to comrades. Duty to country.

When I was thrust into the midst of Desert Storm in 1991, I fully believed my role as a citizen-soldier would help re-establish the freedom and peace of the Kuwaiti people after a brutal invasion by a maniacal dictator-neighbor. It did more than that. As my wartime experience unfolded, I saw that my contribution made a difference to individuals, to a nation, and to the world community.

My first deployment to the Middle East introduced me to the scorching desert, Saddam Hussein, scorpions in your boots, blistering sandstorms, and inedible MREs. But it did not prepare me for Iraq.

I am continually asked by the curious and inquisitive, "So, what was it really like in Iraq?" My answer: My experience in Iraq was magical.

As they try to conceal a look of perplexed disbelief, I can only imagine what they are thinking: "C'mon. Iraq is a hellhole. It's nothing but sweltering heat, endless sand, and crazed extremists whose life ambition is to kill Americans as they blow themselves up."

In the midst of that war-torn inferno they saw on the news every night, I found a spiritual oasis. As enemy mortars shattered nearby hotel walls, Black Hawks thundered overhead, and the crackle of small arms split the night, I discovered a way to carve out some sacred space, a process which changed both Iraq and me forever.

The journey was totally unexpected—oh, I knew I was headed for a war zone. I had done that before. But how could I have known that I would end up close friends with several Iraqi generals? How could I have predicted I would fall in love with Iraqi children? How could I have known my entire future would be determined by a single phone call?

Although the spiritual terrain I traversed was rugged and bleak, my ultimate destination was the oasis I sought. As an Army interrogator, my job was to get inside the heads of Iraqis. The oasis appeared as I looked into their hearts.

There is significant history being forged in Iraq right now. Democracy has been launched. Businesses are opening doors. Capitalism is creating opportunities. Alliances are being formed. Freedom is being tested.

It may be years before this history is taught to children in our schools. This historic saga is unfolding daily as American soldiers bear the torch of freedom to a part of the world where freedom's light has been in short supply. It changed my life to see what a glimmer of light can do for a nation that has struggled in darkness for decades.

Iraqis went out of their way to express appreciation for the work of the Coalition. Iraqi freedom was bought at the supreme price— American soldiers' blood. The Iraqis know it. And they aren't afraid to acknowledge it. *Saving Babylon* is a glimpse into the history of Operation Iraqi Freedom that the American public needs to know.

In 1776, when the Declaration of Independence was first read in public and the Liberty Bell rang out in celebration, one witness said of that famous bell, "It rang as if it meant something." Freedom still means something.

I am continually thankful for the opportunity I had to work side by side with the Iraqi people, watching them discover that freedom has enduring meaning.

Chapter One

A Journey Begins

"Are we going? Am I on the list?"

I could tell by his voice that Sgt. Jensen was getting perturbed with my calls. I couldn't blame him. Like many reservists, I had been contacting the National Guard Armory every day to discover my deployment status.

Tensions in the Middle East were escalating and Saddam Hussein was becoming increasingly belligerent and uncooperative. Military action seemed unavoidable, so most of us in our Military Intelligence (MI) unit fully expected the phone call notifying us of mobilization.

"It's time," said the voice on the phone. "Be ready to move out on the 7th."

Along with the other 150 Utah Army National Guardsmen, all of whom were part of a Military Intelligence Battalion, I had only four days to prepare. I was about to be launched on an unknown mission, to an unfamiliar country, for an undetermined period of time.

Just four days to tie up loose ends at work and at home, pack my essential items, and prepare my family for an extended period of time without me. One day was consumed by the Soldier Readiness Process (SRP), a battery of pre-departure medical, dental, and vision exams to ensure medical readiness. The slug of immunizations and the distribution of medications, antidotes, and mask inserts let me know the nature of the risks awaiting me.

Preparing for deployment was not a new experience for me, having gone through it a decade before during Desert Storm. I knew what to expect each step of the way, recalling with precise detail the mobilization process which would take me again to a Middle East desert with camels, scorpions, sandstorms, heat, and veiled women.

For four days I dashed about as if my life depended on it—and it did—trying to make sure nothing had been forgotten, that family and work issues were settled, and that every possible needed item was packed. Once my mobilization files were in order and personal situations were handled the best they could be, I was ready to leave.

As usual, I packed heavy, going way over limit. If the limit was two boxes, I had four; I knew what I was going to need. I prepared for the worst and hoped for the best.

As I did during Desert Storm, I brought everything I would need to set up my kitchen with all the "fixin's," remembering all too well the awful taste and smell of a daily diet of MREs (meals, ready to eat). My enhancements made MREs ready to enjoy rather than ready to endure.

February 7, 2003, was an especially cold winter day, as we converged at Camp Williams, south of Salt Lake City. As I pulled into the parking lot, a large crowd of people had already formed to support my unit's departure for what was being referred to as an extension of Operation Enduring Freedom, America's war against terror in Afghanistan and elsewhere. The buses were lined up in front of the armory, and friends and family members were milling about like restless cattle before a thunder storm.

Grabbing my bags, with the help of my sons, I ventured over to the buses to load up my gear but was repeatedly stopped by numerous friends who had come out to see me off. With hardly a word being spoken, we embraced, knowing full well what might be in store for us in the days ahead. As I glanced over the crowd, I noticed old military buddies that I had served with in years past as well as some fellow tentmates from the sands of Desert Storm. They were all there to show their support for those of us departing for this new conflict in the Middle East.

I embraced General Tarbet, Adjutant General for the Utah National Guard, who had initiated the call-up. He was the same individual who had called me to the Middle East some 12 years before. Now, with tears in his eyes, he wished me well.

"Good luck, Chief. Wish I could go with you." He echoed the sentiments of others staying behind. "Make sure they all come back alive," he demanded. "And make sure they all keep their head in the game," he ordered, knowing precisely what would be required of us.

I made the rounds to ensure I expressed appreciation to all who had ventured out on a cold February morning, visiting with some I hadn't seen in years. Some were surprised to see me still in uniform departing for yet another life-changing deployment to the Middle East.

"I didn't know you were still in," some said. Those who knew me well knew I would make the most of it. "Glad you are going with them," some expressed. "It will be good to have a few older birds going with the young ones, not yet tempered by the winds of war," one old comrade commented.

My family had not prepared well for the bitter chill of the winter air; my daughter clung to those around her just to stay warm. It was all too familiar. I still had vivid memories of her and the other children clinging to my wife years ago as I drove away on a bus on a cold winter's day, heading off to Desert Storm. Suddenly, I found myself inching onto the bus.

"Goodbye. I love you, Dad." One by one, my kids waved their final farewells. There came a point where I couldn't look back anymore.

"Be safe," was chanted over and over again by all those who were standing near the bus. The diesel engines churned out pungent fumes as weeping family members backed away.

Before I knew it, the bus pulled out. The journey had begun and I was now with my new family—my brothers and sisters of the military. The departure was emotionally afflicting, but my mind was already focused on the serious nature of our mission and the business at hand.

It was a physically and emotionally uncomfortable bus ride to Fort Carson, Colorado Springs, Colorado. Most were still in silent shock over what had just happened. I started a lighthearted movie in the bus to distract us from the images of our sad and crying loved ones, images which were still painfully fresh. I did everything possible to keep things loose and jovial.

We were an exceptional bunch of guys in comparison to typical Reserve units. Most had traveled extensively and many had served as missionaries in various places around the globe. Most were spiritually oriented, with deep roots in faith and family. Our departure from the comforts of civilian life to an unfamiliar and threatening war zone had motivated many to become even more spiritual. As the bus pulled us away from the familiar surroundings of home, our mood was somber but our spirits were high. We were doing all we could to stay positive as we made the best of the situation.

Long bus rides lend themselves to introspection. I found myself pondering my leadership role in what our unit was about to experience. This was one of those times in life when no matter what happened, I was committed to maintaining a positive attitude and making the most of every situation. In my position, as morale officer and chief warrant officer (CW4) and with so many young faces on board, I felt like everyone's father figure. I suspect my graying hair helped solidify that role. Here was an opportunity to be a positive force for change and development in these young soldiers' lives. I silently wondered if the key to success would be improving myself.

Deployment required all of us to be more considerate and more patient with each other. Even though we had not left the United States yet, tensions rose and many became increasingly frustrated with their new life. What might have been a minor social faux pas back home could blow up into a major crisis in this social pressure cooker. It was a difficult situation for many, testing their ability to adapt to the demands of a new life under new and unfamiliar circumstances.

After three weeks at Fort Carson, preparing to become soldiers of war, my unit finally got the call to move out. The message informed us that we would be leaving bright and early Monday morning at "o-dark-hundred." Our commander decided to give us some time off to spend our last stateside weekend with our wives, who had driven hundreds of icy miles to Fort Carson for a final farewell weekend.

"Go do whatever you want. Enjoy yourselves. But be back at the barracks Sunday evening at 1700," the commander ordered. "Say your goodbyes and be ready to move out with all of your gear on the bus by that time." He made it crystal clear that we had to be ready to leave.

I had a great weekend with my wife, spending a couple of nights in a nice hotel, indulging in the local cuisine of Colorado Springs and just being together. However, always close to the surface was one surreal thought: "Before I know it, I will be in Iraq fighting a war."

In the final hours before departure, I couldn't escape thoughts of what I was facing. As a means of pointing that emotional energy in the right direction, I engaged my mind in a pep talk with myself.

I believe in this important mission. Someone has to pay the price for freedom. My efforts will help create a land of freedom and democracy.

> *I have skills that are needed, backed by years of experience, which I can share with others younger than I, who have been called upon for the first time to serve their country and the cause of freedom. I know that what I am doing is important for America, the Iraqi people, and the world.*
>
> *We are about to make history, changing the world forever by removing a tyrant from power. I am ready for whatever is to come, with no fear and no worries. My heart and mind are at peace.*

I was anxious to get over there, get my job done, and get home. Memories of my short three-month stint during Desert Storm filled my mind. "The sooner we all get going the better for everyone," Major Dewey, our company commander, reminded us in our send-off. "It's tough just sitting around waiting for things to happen. We need to get over there, so we can get home sooner." The argument made sense, but my stomach still churned as I thought of heading off to another war zone.

Of course, I fully expected to get over there just to wait around for a while anyway. It wouldn't have been the military without the rushing around punctuated by long periods of waiting. It's kind of like baseball; you wait and wait for something to happen and then everything happens in just a few seconds.

We flew to the Middle East in a large chartered commercial jet, making several stops along the way. Each stop involved hours of waiting. I took every opportunity to keep the atmosphere light and in high spirits. At one time, after joking around with the crew, I was made an honorary flight attendant, pinned and everything. I was in charge of speaking to my troops on the plane over the intercom system, which gave me a chance to really cut up and interject some levity into an otherwise tedious trip.

We landed in Kuwait City around 10 PM. There was not a light in the sky to give me a clue about where I was or what time it was. It was the blackest night I'd ever seen. We were rushed onto several waiting buses with curtains drawn for security, for transport to Camp Wolf, a stone's throw from the landing field.

"MOVE OUT! Quickly, quickly!" the instructions were snapped. "This is not a secured area," claimed the sergeant in charge. Of course, that made us feel right at home. "Keep the curtains closed," was the command. This was the Army. This was war.

Next came the bus ride from Camp Wolf to Camp Udairi, which was something right out of *Raiders of the Lost Ark*. I had never been on such a long and bumpy bus ride in my life. It took almost three hours to get to the base on a 20-lane road through the desert. Actually, there were no lanes, just people driving across the sun-baked desert sands in self-proclaimed lanes, the paved road having ended a short time after our departure.

We were jammed into small Kuwaiti buses with tiny uncomfortable seats, racing through the desert as if we were being chased. Our Indian drivers acted like this was some camel race to see who could get there first. The packs on our backs forced us forward on the seat. We could barely fit half a butt cheek on the seat with two guys per seat. I was catching air off every bump, while our driver ignored all potential road hazards, perhaps to win the undisclosed prize at the finish line.

As we sped into the desert horizon, we continued on past several other U.S. military bases along the way. I noticed that other bases were named after familiar places in the States like Camp New York and Camp Virginia. It was comforting to see words and names I recognized as we sped to our base in the middle of nowhere. Of course, I couldn't help but wonder what Udairi meant—possibly an Arabic term for uninhabitable.

To make the ride even more uncomfortable, I was loaded down with all my military gear—at least 60 pounds of essential equipment that I wouldn't go anywhere without: gas mask, M16 rifle, Kevlar helmet, flak jacket, and chemical suit. But no complaints—I had been issued all this stuff because someone knew I would need it.

Arriving at the base late that night, our check-in took place in the pitch blackness of the desert evening. I was stumbling around in an effort to identify my bags from the rest of our unit's bags that were strewn on the ground. I was then directed to find my way in the unfamiliar darkness to the mess tent. Dinner ended up being two deep fried chicken patties and some rice.

After much difficulty, I figured out which tent I was supposed to be in, which surprisingly hadn't been arranged ahead of time. It was almost as if they weren't expecting the arrival of over a hundred soldiers. I threw my bags in the tent, set up my cot, and crashed on the spot. Gratefully, I slipped into an instantly sound sleep, a deserved reward for the long trip, the time change, and the ordeal I had just been through.

I was living in a large Bedouin-style tent with about 50 other guys. The tent was just like the ones the desert tribes live in; well designed for the desert environment, but not too spacious. Our personal space consisted of an area about six feet wide and six feet long, half of which was taken by the cot. The space around my cot provided room to hang things up and still left a small amount of space for my duffle bags and large black boxes. It wasn't easy to settle into that kind of cramped existence—but I didn't expect to be there too long. I hesitated to take out much of my stuff due to the ever-present Sand Monster. Once the inevitable sand seeped into your stuff, you could never get it out.

With the increasing flow of more troops arriving in camp, our personal space became smaller and smaller. Eventually we were packed in like cordwood. Our allowable personal space had shrunk to the point that everyone was within two feet of another person on each side. In an effort to recapture my shrinking personal space, I decided to go ahead with my idea to build things vertically, allowing me to take advantage of the abundance of space I had above my cot.

I designed and built a piece of furniture that straddled my cot, creating additional shelf space and also providing some protection from the elements. It was perfect. Just what we all needed. Seeing my masterpiece, others wanted to build the same thing for themselves. Anything I could do to improve living conditions helped morale and boosted our spirits, as we adapted to life in that uneasy environment.

In this pre-battle environment, the enemy was sand. I tried to maintain my positive energy, but it was hard to even function with sand blowing everywhere. Our moods went up and down with the surging tide of sand-laden wind, known as *habood* in Arabic. For nearly a week it was oppressively dusty with inescapable sandstorms all day, every day. It is difficult to imagine what these storms are like without experiencing one. The sand blended so fully with the air that I couldn't see in front of my face even inside my tent. It was impossible to keep the grit from invading everything—my weapon, my bags, my tent, my food. At times breathing became a laborious process; with every breath I sucked in sand like a giant vacuum. At times it felt like my lungs were filling up with dirt. I wished I had a dip stick to give me an accurate reading of my sand level.

The particles were extremely fine, almost microscopic, creeping into every unsealed crack and crevice, making my ears and nose easy targets. I remember having to deal with the sand the last time I was in Kuwait, but you never get used to it. I hoped everyday that the wind would stop blowing or at least slow down long enough to make sight a possibility.

In my 12-year absence from the desert I had forgotten how the desert wind blows, throwing its weight around and sandblasting your face with an abrasive furor. It had been blowing since I arrived, without stopping. In some ways it was like a blizzard, but with sand instead of snow. The sand made it hard to carry on a normal existence or even do much of anything except run and hide for cover.

When it was time to eat dinner, all of us were required to suit up in full "battle rattle": kevlar helmet, bulletproof vest, and loaded weapon. I put a scarf around my face so I could breathe without inhaling a suffocating amount of sand. Having grown up around the Great Basin in the western United States, I thought I was adapted to desert life—but not that desert. That place was a pit. I just couldn't imagine why anyone would choose to live there, even the tribal Bedouins who had lived there for centuries. My only temporary consolation was that in spite of the omnipresent sand, the temperatures were still below 100° F. But I knew the soul-scorching heat was coming soon.

Several times the sandstorms blew in while I was visiting one of the dozen or so other tents in our group, causing me to get lost as I ventured back to my tent only a hundred yards away.

One night a group of us, while trying to get back from the mess tent with a plate of food in our hands, encountered a sandstorm that suddenly blew in out of nowhere. The sand made it impossible to see anything in front of us and caused us to become completely disoriented. Like blind sheep, we repeatedly stumbled into barbed wire and other hidden road hazards in the darkness of the sand-filled night. We finally ran into someone with a light who knew the way back to our tents. We felt totally helpless against Mother Nature and her ferocity. The food we were carrying had been abundantly peppered with a layer of inedible grit.

When the sand wasn't blowing, there were moments when I was captivated by the bare beauty and timeless majesty of the desert. On a clear day you really could see forever. The sprawling sky took on a royal hue and the sunsets were extraordinary.

As the sandstorms subsided, simple pleasures like walking outside and taking a deep breath were no longer unthinkable. One morning, before it got too hot, I went for a long run around the berm. The berm is a barricade of sand piled up about 15 feet high around the camp perimeter. If I ran the entire berm area it worked out to about 6 miles, which was a fair distance for me in that hot, dusty, and dangerous environment.

I decided to establish a pattern of daily exercise, with the intention of keeping it up for as long as I was in country. I committed myself to start up a physical training program beginning the next day at 6 AM and every morning thereafter. The physical training kept me ready for any combat requirement. It also kept my emotions in check.

As I ran my route along the berm, I noticed a number of things about the place that felt right—like the hundreds of Apache Longbow helicopters, the best helicopters the military has, lined up on the tarmac. There were also several Patriot Missile batteries set up to protect the Apaches from possible Scud attacks. No photo could capture both the visual and emotional impact of seeing these helicopters and missiles ready to do their duty.

Camp Udairi housed over 9,000 soldiers in the weeks and days leading up to the war. The troop build-up made for long food lines and a shortage of many essentials, especially toilet paper.

Bathroom issues, though never pleasant to think about, really had a significant impact on morale. One camp rule I never broke was to avoid the porta-potty during the hottest part of the afternoon.

To live to go another day,
Never go in the heat of the day.

There were days that outside air temperature climbed to 120° F and the latrines were probably over 140° F. An oven like that squeezed every last drop of perspiration out of you while burning your lungs with the most putrid steam imaginable.

Our location was about 20 miles southeast of the Iraqi border. We knew the plan was to move into Iraq soon. The war plans were aggressive with everyone expecting things to unfold quickly. Everything was pointing towards the war kicking off soon, within days. With our strategic position so close to the Iraqi border, our plan was to move north as fast as possible and to see Coalition troops eventually secure Baghdad.

I had been reading a number of books while at Udairi, which helped me understand the context and purpose of our mission. I

Jeff Hanson checks out a nearly 140° F reading on the outhouse thermometer at Camp Bucca.

knew that some of the people back home didn't understand or didn't agree with the war, but it was the only way to free these people from a dangerous, merciless, and ruthless leader. Saddam Hussein had killed thousands of his own people and would not hesitate to give his weapons of mass destruction to a terrorist organization or to use them himself, which he had done in the past.

I received my new assignment and a briefing on what our plans for action would be once the war started. I was assigned to work in the Battalion Tactical Operation Center (TOC), which was over Company A, where most of our people were assigned. My task was to manage the flow of reports and information that came in from the interrogation teams in the field and to publish those through all intelligence channels.

As real intelligence responsibilities began to materialize—coding documents, interrogating captives, deciphering messages—we knew that we were going to have to get reliable assistance from translators that could be trusted. Locating, hiring, and training Arabic translators was essential to successful intelligence gathering. My fluency in Korean would not be helpful in this war.

Meeting the Iraqi civilian interpreters from the U.S., almost twenty of them, was encouraging. They seemed intelligent, educated, and anxious to participate. They were hired to assist our group of interrogators in conducting interrogations in Arabic.

My discussions with the interpreters were not only fascinating, but they confirmed what I had read and heard about the situation in Iraq. All the interpreters were anxious for us to go north and take out Saddam's government, freeing the Iraqi people from the "wicked regime," as they put it. They made it evident that the Iraqi people had suffered greatly under Saddam's rule.

The accounts which the Iraqi interpreters related to me were both astounding and shocking. Our discussions revealed unthinkable atrocities Saddam had committed against his own people. He had been killing and torturing using gas and chemical weapons repeatedly throughout the last 20 years, either on the neighboring Iranians or the Kurdish minority within Iraq. Everyone knew he had weapons of mass destruction and past experience had shown he would not hesitate to use them.

In our initial meetings, I tried to build a relationship with the interpreters, in hopes that I would become familiar with each of them personally before being thrust into an interrogation together. I needed to know, to some degree, each individual's personality, prejudices, and thinking process, which could interfere with or support my interrogation methods. Also, for more selfish reasons, befriending them would provide a means to get real food once a week when they were able to leave for Kuwait City on a weekly shopping spree. Fresh vegetables and fruits were like gold around camp—ingredients totally absent from our daily diet. I wanted to try some local cuisine, too, if I had the chance. Bring on the hummus and flatbread!

Chapter Two

Shock and Awe

We all expected the start of military action to happen any day. Personally, I expected the all-out assault on Saddam to launch by mid-March and the tension was building to a crescendo as the days seemed to creep by. In that environment of ambiguous anticipation, time passed slowly.

We had been reviewing the impressive war plans in the TOC, as D-day got closer and closer. "It's going to be quite an amazing show of military might and technology; you just won't believe it," our commanding officer explained. We understood that the major phase of the war would begin with intense aerial attacks on Baghdad and other cities. This overwhelming barrage, publicized in advance by the Pentagon, was meant to instill "shock and awe."

On Tuesday, March 18, we woke up to the news that President Bush had given Saddam and his sons 48 hours to give up power and go into exile or face invasion by more than a 170,000 Coalition troops poised on Iraq's borders. "Their refusal to do so," said the President, "will result in military conflict commenced at a time of our choosing."

We had spent nearly two months actively preparing for this exact moment. But the President's declaration that "all the decades of deceit and cruelty have now reached an end," let the men and women of the military know that our job was about to begin.

In the days leading up to the ultimatum, our preparations and readiness continued to intensify. And yet, much of the routine of life at Camp Udairi remained in a state of rigorous anticipation. By the morning of Thursday, March 20, Saddam had less than 18 hours remaining on his 48-hour ultimatum. We had been playing our own version of beach volleyball that morning, when we were told that there would be an address broadcast from President Bush to the American people. Appropriately, we stopped our game to hear what the President had to say.

"On my orders, Coalition forces have begun striking selected targets of military importance to undermine Saddam Hussein's ability to wage war." Then speaking to the United States military personnel in the Middle East, the President continued with solemn resolve: "The peace of a troubled world and the hopes of an oppressed people now depend on you. That trust is well placed."

To our surprise, in an address that lasted only four minutes, the President launched the war ahead of schedule—at least ahead of our schedule, surprising even our leaders. In spite of the surprise timing, everyone was prepared to launch the offensive and move toward the freeing of the Iraqi people.

The words of the President connected with the conviction of every soldier present at Camp Udairi that morning: "This will not be a campaign of half measures, and we will accept no outcome but victory.... We will bring freedom to others and we will prevail."

It seemed that even before the President's speech was over reports of Tomahawk Cruise missiles being launched towards Baghdad were streaming in. We learned later that air raid sirens, flashes of light and U.S. warplanes had decorated the early morning skies of Baghdad starting at 6:34 AM.

Everyone had expected the war to kick off in the evening, the trump card being our superior night-fighting capabilities. So it came as somewhat of a surprise that the war started during early morning daylight hours. But the timing made sense given the nature of the targets. Coalition aircraft would instantly bomb military targets to soften up the country's defenses against a broader air and ground attack. Instead of focusing on the demolition of Iraqi forces and factories, the objective would be to cripple the enemy's will to fight.

An early morning surprise attack with hundreds of smart bombs raining down on military and leadership targets would paralyze the country. Iraqi commanders would be cut off from their divisions. Forces in the field would be cowed by an enemy they couldn't see, and the Iraqi regime would assume early on that defeat was imminent and inevitable. This was the essence of our shock-and-awe strategy.

Many of the regular Army soldiers I lived with had been there since November 2002, arriving many months before hostilities began. I could only imagine how they must have felt. Many of them came right from duty in Afghanistan, interrogating prisoners during Operation Enduring Freedom. Those soldiers, along with many of us, were just tired of waiting for something to move either way; waiting can demoralize those who just want to accomplish their mission and go home. The events of March 20, 2003, let us know the wait was over.

The kind of war we originally expected began that evening. The sun set on Baghdad at 6:15 PM on March 20. At about 9:05 PM, U.S. planes unleashed their muscle on military targets in central Baghdad. Explosions were reported close to the Royal Palace, the ministry of defense, and the Al-Rasheed Airport in the western part of the city. Within the first 24 hours of the war, U.S. forces planned to light up Iraq with more than 1,500 bombs and missiles.

By 11 PM that evening, damage assessments were starting to pour in. One of Saddam's palaces had been destroyed. A residential compound in Baghdad where Saddam, his sons, and other key leaders may have been hiding was hit. An intelligence service headquarters and a Republican Guard facility had been severely hit. Heavy bombing also hit Tikrit, Saddam's family home, as well as the cities of Mosul and Kirkuk in the north.

The enemy was particularly busy the first night, launching missiles every hour all night long. Not all of them were Scuds, but unless we knew otherwise, we all reacted as if they were. The process was simple. Whenever an alert was heard, depending on the type of alert, we got our masks on and moved to the bunker. I considered moving my cot into the bunker so I wouldn't have to wake up, but it was my job to make sure that everyone was ready and that no one was having any problems getting their equipment on. We knew what Saddam Hussein was capable of doing and we just couldn't take any unnecessary chances.

The Scud missile is a Russian-made, surface-to-surface missile system with a range of about 300 miles. The most threatening aspect of a Scud is its dumb unpredictability. The warhead can be explosive, chemical, or nuclear, and they have notoriously poor accuracy as they coast unguided to the target area.

Once the war started, our base was on alert for any Iraqi missiles launched in our direction. As soon as one was launched, the military knew the direction in which it was headed. This gave us sufficient advance warning to jump into our chemical protective gear, run into a bunker, and wait for the "all clear" sound to go off. For the first few days of the war we spent much of our time jumping in and out of bunkers and donning chemical protective suits, called MOPP gear. Since we were never sure about the nature of the Scud missiles being launched in our direction, we took every precaution. Better safe than sorry.

Black Hawk and Apache helicopters were lined up ready to depart on their nightly missions of seek and destroy. Camp Udairi was an airbase, with hundreds of helicopters of all sizes and shapes, loaded down with all types of weaponry. It was quite a sight seeing them positioned on the tarmac, ready for action.

The Apache is the Army's attack helicopter complete with Hellfire missiles, rockets, and a 30mm chain gun. Its strong suit is versatility as it delivers precision strikes in day, night, and adverse weather conditions. With a combat mission speed of 167 mph and a range of 300 miles these birds could be employed at a moment's notice around the clock.

The Black Hawk is a utility tactical transport helicopter capable of transporting a fully equipped infantry squad faster and in a wider range of weather conditions than its UH-1 "Huey" predecessor.

Both the Apache and the Black Hawk are amazing birds, unmatched by anything else in the world. I stopped during my runs around the berm on many occasions to talk with the pilots, crew, and engineers who worked on them doing maintenance. I was extremely curious and was consistently enthralled by the capabilities of our machines and equipment.

One night I went outside during one of the missile attacks just to observe the fireworks. I was able to hear the sound of artillery pounding away at Iraqi positions. All night long I could hear the sound of helicopters departing for their nightly missions.

Starting Thursday morning and continuing for the first few days of the war, Iraq was still capable of launching their Scud missiles against U.S. troops in Kuwait. And given our position, size, and air base status, I knew we were prime targets at Udairi.

Our star defender was the new Patriot surface-to-air guided missile defense system. Its Gulf War predecessor was designed to explode near slow-moving targets like aircraft, but was never intended to shoot down ballistic missiles. The new version of the Patriot is equipped with a hit-to-kill technology and is capable of intercepting Scuds at a higher altitude than was possible back in

Patriot missle launcher on the ready.

1991. The interceptor would collide with the Iraqi missile like a bullet hitting a bullet. The exploding warhead is capable of destroying incoming Iraqi warheads, including any nuclear, chemical, or biological agents.

One evening I was able to witness one of these Patriots in action. With batteries located on our base, about 200 yards from my tent, I could hear the unmistakable sound of the Patriot's launch. I ran outside in my chemical suit and stared at the distant sky waiting for the hit. Instantly, a bright flash appeared signaling the Patriot had met its target. Seconds later the sound of the collision could be heard, confirming success. We returned to our tents resting a little more peacefully.

Our Patriot missiles went down on occasion while needed repairs were made. You can imagine my feelings one night when I got an email saying our base was not going to be protected by Patriots for a while. It was a good thing no one else knew about that, like the Iraqi Army. That would have ruined my day for sure.

It was a strange feeling to be out in the desert late at night with a war going on all around me, knowing that people just like me were at that moment putting their lives in harm's way and even dying. People's lives were changing on both sides and things would never be the same again for any of us.

While I was standing there I could feel the concussion of each artillery shell being shot. There was a jolt and a push of air from the force of the explosion. The dust was stirred up all night long as the helicopters went out and back, leaving on missions and returning minutes or hours later. I prayed for those young men, who were risking their lives that night, flying into the depths of danger and returning to do it again another day.

I continued in my responsibilities at the battalion's TOC. I made sure all of our teams got out on the right assignments and then assisted in managing the flow of intelligence and information from these teams. I was also assisting with arrangements to move the Joint Interrogation Facility (JIF) northward into Iraq, when the time came.

We recognized that the key to finding the "smoking guns," as the weapons of mass destruction were sometimes called, was intelligence gathering. To that end, we shouldered the responsibility for getting out accurate and timely reports to all of the intelligence channels and agencies.

I spent most of my days in the TOC, which was the command center for our MI unit. This was where all the planning was done and where all the incoming intelligence arrived. We enabled everyone who needed it to have access to the most up-to-date information on what was happening in the war.

As early as March 21, the second day of the war, a top Iraqi military commander along with his top deputy and thousands of troops, surrendered to U.S. forces. On one of these early days of the war a couple of Iraqi generals were captured, causing me to be busily engaged in lining up the interrogators to be flown to where the generals were being held.

Our group of MI soldiers was getting new missions daily as the need arose to question captured POWs. As various cities were taken by Coalition forces, many of the Iraqi commanders were surrendering, with their whole units capitulating.

With the word that several teams were leaving Camp Udairi in the morning, I went across the way to visit with fellow soldiers from my Utah unit, to say goodbye to those leaving on what was called Team Wheeler, a Mobile Interrogation Team (MIT). I gave them some last minute advice and took a moment to have a team prayer. Five of them would be leaving in the morning to go to where several high-ranking Iraqi officers were being held by the Marines. They would be crossing the berm and traveling into the war zone, into an area that had just been taken by our rapidly advancing forces.

It was about 10 PM and I was in my tent getting ready to bed down for the night. Most everyone was already asleep, having retired earlier in the evening in expectation of another night of Scud alarms, which could have kept us up all night. There were a few men playing cards on a makeshift table with their gas masks close by. The evening air was rather cool, which was strange but welcome. The night sky had an unusual haze, which was creating an eerie ring around the rising moon just above the horizon. It was extremely dark, which was good news for the night raids that had been planned.

Of the many technological advantages held by the U.S. military, the one most fortuitously suited to this war was our night-fighting capability. All of our soldiers, tanks, armored troop carriers, and aircraft were equipped with night-vision capability which effectively turned the night battlefield into day. Additionally, all of our front-line troops were equipped with a laser target marker fitted to their rifles. At the touch of a button, a red laser dot is placed on the target showing exactly where the bullet will hit when the trigger is pulled.

Our uniquely superior night-vision capability enabled our troops to fight in the cooler night air and maintain an overwhelming combat advantage. Tanks and self-propelled artillery also perform better at night than in the scorching desert heat. Helicopter pilots prefer night combat since the more dense night air provides more bite for the rotors to get into.

Sunday provided the opportunity for me to attend church for about an hour, which was just what I needed. It gave me and the other soldiers who went the chance to get our heads spiritually refocused. It was a welcome break to have time to meditate and pray.

As I walked back to my tent following the services, I had much to reflect on. My feelings about the war began to take on a spiritual

Sunday religious services at Camp Udairi.

tone. I had a feeling I was part of a bigger plan, one that was divinely developed, one that had something to do with blessing the Iraqi people. My mind and heart were open to the promptings of the Spirit—the "still small voice" spoken of by Isaiah, the Old Testament prophet—which enabled me to comprehend the importance of our presence in Iraq and the seriousness of our mission.

Most nights, I stayed up late reading and writing in my journal, getting to bed around midnight, and then immediately falling fast asleep. I generally slept soundly and peacefully in my desert tent, except for the interruptions of nightly Scud alerts. But even when I was awakened by a Scud alert and a subsequent Patriot interception, I was able to quickly return to a deep sleep.

There had been a consistent string of nerve-jangling alerts during the first week of the war, several every day. Sometimes it was just a gas alert, letting me know that I should put my mask on. Other times it was an all-out alert to get to a bunker or bomb shelter. It was reassuring to know that when a missile had been launched in my direction, that a Patriot missile was launched to intercept in response. We had no verified reports of a Scud arriving at its intended destination. All were remarkably intercepted by our friend the Patriot.

One night I was awakened by an unexpected incident that was more disturbing than the routine Scud alerts. At another camp close by, one of our own disgruntled soldiers threw grenades into three tents, including the commander's tent, killing one individual and injuring 13. The grisly incident was widely reported by both the U.S. and worldwide media. It was a tragic event to have one of our own turn against his fellow soldiers.

Although the winds and sandstorms continued making life difficult for all of us, I had gotten used to them to some degree. I found that the best way to deal with them was to avoid them. So I tried to stay inside my work area, where it was somewhat dust free. In the TOC we had a special kind of tent equipped with its own filtration system. This kept us fairly well sealed off, and kept out most of the dust in order to protect the computers.

Although we had access to televised CNN and FOX News, along with BBC radio news, the best and most reliably informative part of my day was the morning briefing. Every morning I could be found waiting for the morning briefing to begin. It was encouraging to receive these updates on what was happening in the war and the news was generally very good.

On day two of the war, Coalition forces were already making impressive strides on the ground, traveling over 100 miles into Iraq from our positions in Kuwait. Bradley Fighting Vehicles and Abrams tanks were rolling unimpeded toward Baghdad in a wave of steel nearly 20 miles long. By March 23, just four days into the war, we had secured several major cities and ports in the south.

Our forces were moving well and making good time as they approached Baghdad. The real trick was to keep our supply lines open and secured, allowing our support team to get supplies through to our advancing forces. One day we got word that a small unit was ambushed and a few people killed. That was disheartening. But over-all the early days of the operation had been very successful with few Coalition casualties.

The news media made it sound like the military was getting bogged down, but that was definitely not the case. There was a lot the media didn't follow, didn't know, and didn't report, even with embedded reporters. All too often the media seemed to focus on the incident when things went wrong. But those were isolated and did not represent the totality of what was really happening.

There was an abundance of rumors and outright lies floating around which were snatched up by overzealous reporters looking for the "big story." I was generally skeptical and occasionally sickened by the way the media outlets were portraying the war. They had such a shortsighted view of things and the notion that it was all supposed to be played out in a few days. I suspect that this approach actually worked in our favor at times, knowing the enemy was also watching the news.

In spite of what the media were or were not reporting, the war continued to progress as planned with many operational and battle-field successes. With less than ten days of war under our belt, we had over 100,000 Coalition forces inside Iraq. That feat alone was evidence of phenomenal success.

In a society driven by instant gratification and sitcom crises which are all resolved in 22 minutes, many Americans expected that this war would also roll out in some sort of fast-forward mode. But for those of us in the military, this was not a video game or television episode. We saw ourselves literally on the stage of history and engaged in a cause which will be validated many years after a reporter files his story.

While standing in the line for chow one day, I was surprised to see FOX News reporter Geraldo Rivera. He was in line to get some of that good Army grub just like me, so I said "Hi," and talked to him for a few minutes. As usual the line was moving slowly, enabling one of the soldiers to run back to his tent and bring back his camera before Geraldo got through the line. I took some pictures with him and chatted a bit about his purpose for being there. I told him I appreciated the fact that he was putting himself in harm's way to get the news and that his support for the troops really meant a lot. He smiled and nodded as he loaded his plate.

I relished my fleeting brush with celebrity, but as soon as I looked at what I was being fed, I was quickly thrust back into the reality of military life.

Reports from Iraqi POWs were starting to come in at an increasing rate. There were reports of captured documents, captured locations, and captured equipment—all of which pointed to our success. A great deal of valuable intelligence was being gathered which helped greatly in winning the war and proving to the world what Saddam had been up to.

More and more information was flowing in about what the Iraqis were doing to their own people to force them to fight against the oncoming Coalition forces. Rumors were spreading about how the Iraqis had started shooting their own soldiers and even civilians on the spot if they wouldn't fight. I also heard stories of kidnappings in which children were abducted and their fathers coerced to fight in exchange for the child's release. I was deeply troubled by the way the Iraqis continued to use hospitals, churches, and mosques as fronts for their military operations.

Some Iraqi soldiers put on our uniforms to disguise themselves as Americans. They were able to initially fool some Coalition troops, getting close enough to begin firing on them and killing several. The next day, to disable that strategy, soldiers put on their rubberized desert-camouflage chem pants to distinguish themselves from any Iraqi soldier masquerading as an American. There were also reports of Iraqi commanders shooting anyone who surrendered, in a desperate attempt to create fear and uncertainty in the minds of their soldiers.

One report from Marines stationed at a checkpoint near Najaf revealed the mind set of the enemy and their disregard for human life. As an Iraqi van was moving through a Marine checkpoint, the Marines motioned to the van to stop several times, but the van just kept on moving through the checkpoint without making any effort to stop. The Marines had ample justification to shoot since just two days earlier in Najaf, five U.S. soldiers were killed when a suicide bomber attacked a checkpoint. Finally, the Marines, having no other choice given the incidents of suicide bombings, opened fire on the van. As they approached the wreckage, they discovered they had shot seven women and children hidden in the back.

The Iraqi military had done this deliberately so they could broadcast to the world that Americans were killing innocent women and children. Iraqis had also been strapping women and children to the outside of vehicles in order to safely cross bridges and roads.

People that accused the U.S. military of killing innocent women and children have no understanding of the extent to which we went to deliberately avoid such loss. The U.S. military, at times to our own detriment, went out of our way to avoid the loss of innocent people— even when we knew the enemy would never use such measures to protect our civilians or even their own wives and children. Never in the history of the U.S. military have we been so committed to minimizing collateral damage in all operations.

There is a price for freedom, known all too well by the men and women on the front lines who are willing to pay it. Death is expected as a part of this struggle. Lives have been lost here, but very few in comparison to other military actions around the world. Fortunately, the United States has the might, the technology and the firepower to minimize the loss of lives on both sides. Every precautionary measure was taken to insure that the fewest lives were lost on both sides. From the information gathered, the Iraqis were amazed at the precision of our weaponry, to the point that many Iraqi civilians were not alarmed by our bombing of governmental locations.

Every day more intelligence on Saddam was surfacing. It confirmed what we had long heard about what a terrible tyrant he had been. I was sickened by the stories of what he had done to his own people, to the Kurdish people, and to our soldiers who were their POWs.

These and other reports provided a stark contrast as I compared the way we treated our POWs and the way they treated theirs. Even when considering the unfortunate events at the Abu Ghraib Prison, there remain striking and fundamental discrepancies between the two systems.

From my experiences of the past 34 years as an interrogator in the U.S. Army, I can speak with substantial authority and firsthand experience about the measures taken by U.S. military to insure the well being of our POWs. Part of our battle plan took into account our responsibility to clothe, feed, and provide necessary medical treatment for our POWs. We were all disturbed by the cruelty and inhumane practices conducted by the Iraqi military.

Based on all the intelligence that was being gathered, I was starting to get a real sense of what it must have been like to live under such a brutal dictator. It must have been terrifying to live with the constant fear that at any moment, for the slightest reason, you or someone in your family could be shot, kidnapped, imprisoned, or killed—and thousands were. Saddam had created an unbelievably elaborate system to insure his own survival and longevity. He was obsessed with his own security, watching everyone and everything, with organizations to watch organizations and other organizations to watch them.

Saddam had perfected a vile art of being deceitful, brutal, cruel, and oppressive, all done so he could subdue his people and remain in complete control. His horrifying and vicious reign was built on evil intentions and selfish aspirations.

Outside my tent, I could see the orange glow of burning oil wells tinting the evening sky. By day, the smoke and dark haze on the distant horizon hung as a reminder of a tyrant obsessed with maintaining his brutal grip on the resources and people of Iraq.

There was an unfortunate incident at Camp Udairi involving a few friends of mine in our unit. They were standing in line to enter the PX, when a small truck sped up and turned the vehicle in their direction. Everyone assumed the driver would turn away but to their surprise he just kept coming, with the obvious intent to kill or injure those in line. The driver was an Egyptian in civilian clothes who was deliberately trying to run down Americans.

Several of those in line were unaware of the approaching vehicle and were hit. One of my good friends, Specialist Conan "Baghdaddy" Heimdal, was hit from behind, flipping him up onto the hood of the truck, smashing his body into the windshield, and then fortunately throwing him away from the truck as it hit a ditch in the sand. A total of six people were hit by the crazed driver who immediately came under fire by those remaining in line, hitting the driver with several bullets. The driver survived and was taken into custody by the military police. Fortunately, no one was seriously hurt, but Baghdaddy did end up with several ruptured disks in his back and a Purple Heart.

The majority of our MI group had plans to move further north, closer to Baghdad, in a few days. Our teams had been going out daily, flying into areas to either interrogate POWs or analyze captured enemy documents and equipment.

Every evening about 9 PM, before retiring for the night, I visited the other tents to give an update on what had transpired in the war that day. Being privy in the TOC to all the latest intelligence, I reviewed the events of the day and discussed what I thought would happen next. Everyone enjoyed this time spent together discussing the details of our military activities.

By April 1, just 13 days into the war, and sooner than expected, our forces reached the outskirts of Baghdad, 19 miles from the center of the city. This progress pleased the war planners, I am sure. But it

Waiting out a Scud alert.

also placed our troops inside the Red Zone where Saddam was most likely to use his chemical weapons. There would also be several days of waiting on the outskirts before launching the Battle of Baghdad. This gave us time to secure our ground positions and to batter Baghdad military and leadership targets with our air power.

I was still quite apprehensive about what was really going on, not sure where Saddam was or what he might resort to. Our frontline forces had not encountered the stiff resistance they expected, even from the Republican Guard, Saddam's most elite force.

One night back at Udairi there was a double whammy—a missile alert coupled with our favorite, the "chemical alert." This put me into MOPP-4, forcing me to put on all my gear *and* my chemical suit. I was totally covered from head to toe and looked like I had been stuffed into some oversized sausage casing. I ran for my 40-foot metal container bomb shelter, which doubles as a sauna with temperatures well above 90°F. I was sure this was part of the Army's new weight-loss program, as my rubber boots filled up with sweat from every pore of my body.

During these first two weeks of the war, I was working 12-hour shifts processing incoming intelligence with no days off. In the face of this demanding schedule, I still took time to reflect upon my second mobilization to a war in the Middle East. I contemplated the value and scope of my contribution as an American soldier and citizen of the world and became increasingly aware that my personal effort and that of my unit was helping to save lives and shorten the length of this war.

This was not about us, but about the Iraqi people. Our success in this conflict would bring freedom to an oppressed nation. Iraqis had lived in fear for so many years that it had become a way of life for them. The silent majority had been forced into submission by the brutal extremes of a dictator bent on securing his tyrannical rule.

I knew the outcome of this war would not rely entirely on the technology, superiority, or the might of the U.S. military. A mightier power was guiding us in this battle. Like our Commander in Chief, I knew that "an angel still rides in the whirlwind and directs this storm." I sensed the hand of the Lord guiding the affairs of this war and knew that with my contribution, a few more of His children would know freedom.

Chapter Three

Out of the Sand Box

It was April 6 and we were 18 days into the war. Our forces had already isolated Baghdad and had closed off the major roads into the city. In a taunting display of military might, our tanks made a brief foray into a Baghdad suburb, crossing the city limits for the first time. To the south, Iraqi forces had lost control of Basra after columns of British troops poured into Iraq's second largest city.

After a long and tiring day, having just laid my head on my pillow, I was wakened by my commander. Expecting news about the war, I was startled to hear him informing me of my mother's death. She had passed away unexpectedly in her sleep the previous night. I was so shocked to hear the news that I couldn't find the words to respond. I sat there stunned and speechless.

Instantly, a flood of emotions ran through my heart. Most of all, I felt so robbed that she had left before I could say one last goodbye. But death doesn't always give us a warning call or a heads up before it strikes. The war reminded me of that daily. I was always close to my mother, a kind and gentle woman; we continued to have a warm and loving relationship throughout my adult years.

I wrestled with what I should do as there were some troublesome choices. Through a satellite phone call that evening I was able to speak with my sister about mom's passing and the immediate steps required of me for her funeral and other arrangements. My sister coaxed me to stay in Iraq to finish my work there, promising she would take care of mother's affairs. She obviously understood me quite well, knowing my feelings about duty, responsibility, and honor. Even so, I knew I would not be able to stay in Iraq. The Army expected me, as they would any other soldier, to return home to handle this pressing family crisis.

That night, sleep was neither a priority nor an option. As I sorted through my gear, my mind filled with thoughts of my mother and a lifetime of tender memories. I went outside for a moment and looked up into the desert sky with tear-filled eyes, to express my love for her, knowing she would be listening. I wanted to be star-struck by the desert night one more time. Locking my sights on the Big Dipper, which in turn pointed to the North Star, my passion to go north to Baghdad was charged.

It didn't take me long to pack up my gear, with most of it being left behind. By dawn my stuff was packed in preparation to board a convoy going south to Camp Doha in Kuwait City. I was scheduled to leave at 10 AM, so I wasn't in a big rush.

Right before leaving, while I was waiting for the vehicles to arrive, about 60 of my men and co-workers came out to say their goodbyes. I was overwhelmed by their expression of concern. Many of the soldiers openly expressed their love for me. I really loved those men and will never forget them. Right as I was leaving, my commander Major Price came out. He took me aside and told me I was his strength and that he would miss me greatly. It was an emotional departure as I waved goodbye to the desert and all that I had become accustomed to.

Our convoy crossed the desert to Camp Doha, where I would catch a connecting bus to the airport. I would depart from Kuwait City on a military transport that evening. With all of the expected stops en route, the military milk run would have me back in Salt Lake City within three days.

I was in a state of complete uncertainty and jumbled emotions. I had no idea when I would be returning to the sand box. I had mixed feelings about leaving the Middle East before my job was done, but I also felt a deep sense of responsibility to support my family at this time of great loss.

My MI unit was ready to move north where the new focus of our work would take place. I desperately wanted to be a part of that new assignment. We were prepared to transition effectively into our new responsibility in Iraq. My departure was an abrupt derailment of the mission I came to perform.

Strangely enough, I was already missing that sand-encrusted wasteland and the people I rubbed shoulders with on a daily basis. Our troops were poised on Baghdad's perimeter and I was not there to finish the fight.

I consoled myself as I pondered what the experience had taught me so far. I was a better person for the experience, viewing myself and my life's purpose differently. I appreciated the little things in life even more. I hoped to never forget the feelings, experiences, and memories washing over me as I returned home to my family.

My return to the States occurred just as the war effort was reaching a dramatic climax. With U.S. forces driving north and encircling Baghdad, there had been many compelling stories of heroism, sacrifice, and concern for the Iraqi people. But I was still filled with apprehension and uncertainty, knowing that the looming Battle of Baghdad would bring different and unexpected challenges.

In the early days of the war, Mobile Interrogation Teams (MIT) and Mobile Exploitation Teams (MET) were sent up north for short periods of time on vital intelligence gathering missions. We were facing a flood of information which expanded daily. Ours was the daunting work of processing this data for the intelligence community.

Our intelligence work was like putting together a jigsaw puzzle. There were so many pieces of this puzzle which seemed to be connecting in front of us as our troops moved toward Baghdad. Each new wave of incoming intelligence was like having another 500-piece puzzle added to the mix of partially connected pieces. There was always more to connect to an ever-expanding puzzle.

It was mind-boggling to contemplate the amount of information that needed to be dug up and the sheer number of people that needed to be interrogated. As we interviewed people about what had been going on in Iraq, we were deluged with accounts of atrocities shared by Iraqi citizens now that the floodgates had finally been opened.

Even at this early stage of the war, a clear picture was emerging of Saddam's reign of terror, which was marked by heartless brutality and genocidal outbursts. For me, I didn't really care if the weapons of mass destruction were ever found. Saddam was an international fugitive and a war criminal. Twenty-five years of Saddam's tyranny had torn apart a nation and disrupted the entire region.

Just before my departure, half of our MI unit, as the advance party, moved north toward Baghdad to prepare the site for the rest who would be joining them later. This advance party would be in Iraq for some time, gathering information and intelligence before the rest of our unit assembled at that advanced location.

For our unit, the waiting was over. Our mission was now beginning. It was time for us to take center stage and do what we were sent to do. I was mentally prepared to go the distance and committed to seeing this through. But as the jet lifted off the runway leaving Kuwait in the distance, I felt the responsibility of unfinished business. By leaving before my mission was completed, it seemed I was breaking faith with my men and turning my back on what needed to be done to insure their safe return.

Home time is different from Army time. Home has a more predicable, manageable pace, one with a fair amount of autonomy. Army life, on the other hand, is highly structured, but you spend much of the time in suspense. Then once something happens, you don't always understand the motive, rationale, or outcome. Waiting has always been a familiar feature of military life, which can lead to serious boredom.

Many of the soldiers in Kuwait had been there since November 2002, waiting for the war and their jobs to begin. The preparation and waiting time turned into days, weeks, and months of doing not much of anything. I saw soldiers react to boredom differently. In fact, how they used their free time was often a more telling test than experiences on the front lines. The real character of a man seems to come out when he has nothing to do.

Some soldiers spent their time worrying about when they were going home or how long they were going to be there, or what they were going to do tomorrow. They spent too much time discussing what every order meant, forever trying to figure out the underlying politics of any action and reading between the lines, as if they were going to discover some hidden meaning that might help them make sense of everything. That just doesn't happen in the Army.

There were also those that complained about everything. Being an arm-chair general made them feel superior to everyone else, at least for the moment. They continuously looked for ways to find fault with things, which was easy to do in the Army.

I decided to take charge of my own environment and exert control over those things that were within my sphere of influence. I saw every experience as an opportunity. To make my stay in the Middle East worthwhile, I had to create my own opportunities. There was nothing to be gained by worrying, criticizing or complaining. It was within my power to choose how to respond to any situation. I had the ability to select my direction and to choose my outcome. That had always been my approach while serving in the Army, and if I was to return, I expected to maintain that perspective.

It wasn't hard to reacquaint myself with the comforts of home life; I enjoyed them so much. I took special notice of simple things like a comfortable chair, hot water from the tap, and a thermostat to set my home temperature wherever I wanted it to be. Americans live in such luxury and comfort compared to so many places in the world.

As soothing as the comforts of home were, I couldn't escape the images of my life in a tent with all of the gear and equipment, cramping my style and limiting my space. Clotheslines were strung throughout the tent and we sat on handcrafted makeshift furnishings. My individual space consisted of my cot, my cot-straddling shelf, and a small table at the end of the cot that extended out into the middle of the tent. I was able to sit on my cot and write or type on the table.

To the left of my cot I had put down a couple of prayer rugs to give my feet a soft resting place. Most of the time, I'd remove my boots and run around barefoot in the tent, enjoying the soft feeling of the rugs on the bottom of my feet. I had a small table wedged between my cot and the one next to mine. On the surface of this table I had drilled holes, into which a variety of cups could be placed, like drink holders. My clothes were hung up behind me on the roping of the tent, each article hung inside a plastic bag to keep out the ever-encroaching sand. Each morning I folded up my bedding, placed it under the cot-straddling shelf, and draped a poncho over all my gear.

Even though I was at a comfortable and safe distance from my tent in Camp Udairi, I couldn't put those memories away. I had gone home to fulfill the needs of my family, to offer a eulogy at my mother's funeral, and to handle the many details following her death. The days which followed brought many difficult circumstances as well as some tender and trying times. It was right for me to be there.

On the other hand, I knew I had unfinished business in Iraq. There was still a mission at hand. And my desire to complete that mission with my men was still burning bright.

Chapter Four

A Home Called Bucca

After three weeks of civilian life, my orders came to return to the Middle East. By May 7, 2003, I was back in the sand. While I was gone, the toppling of Saddam had become quite literal as U.S. Marines helped a crowd of Iraqis pull down a massive statue of the dictator in the heart of Baghdad. Widespread looting, lawlessness, and general chaos followed. Throughout the country Iraqi Army divisions surrendered or instantly disbanded as U.S. troops restored order to places like Tikrit, Mosul, and Kirkuk. Those of us in MI had a mounting supply of work with the daily capture, defection or surrender of generals, government ministers, Baath Party leaders, and other characters whose faces appeared on the deck of playing cards featuring our most wanted suspects.

It was both a peculiar and familiar feeling coming back to the desert. Sure, there were a few days of readjustment; reintroduction to sand, wind, heat—and the war. Many of my good friends had moved on to other assignments, to fulfill other missions. It was strange to see the camp so empty, with almost everyone I knew gone. My unit had been spread out all over Iraq on variety of missions.

From the moment I arrived back at camp there was a stream of long days working into the late hours of the night, generating and editing reports from MI assets in the field on critical issues. When I arrived at my tent around 11:30 PM, most people were already fast asleep. It's not easy trying to fall asleep to the sound of 40 guys snoring all at once. Fortunately, the constant humming of the generator outside the tent muffled the roar of snoring soldiers.

The intelligence flow was steadily increasing in the early weeks of the war, bringing in more and more valuable information about people, places, and events of interest. The pieces of this puzzle were all coming together as our team of interrogators continued to interview POWs and other detainees.

In my short absence there had been many changes, not the least of which was the increasing heat. Many mornings I was awakened abruptly by sweat running down the middle of my back and was surprised to see the temperature in the tent had already reached over 100° F.

Fortunately, temperatures fell quickly in the evening, cooling to a bearable temperature for sleeping. Of course, it was still springtime and too early to know what the heat of summer had in store.

One new addition to camp was an increasing insect population sharing our tent. The flying bugs were especially attracted to the light of my computer screen. They swarmed around my head as if at any moment they were going to launch their assault and take over my computer.

With the increasing temperature came a cool amenity—ice. Our camp now had ice deliveries on a daily basis, which really improved the quality of life. Each morning a truck with a big semi-trailer full of ice made the rounds, passing out ice to the troops at each stop along the way. We dug a pit outside our tent and lined it with Styrofoam hoping to keep the ice from melting the minute it was received.

The nights were unusually calm, with nothing more than a slight cooling breeze drifting across the desert floor. There was a reassuring calm and certain serenity to the desert on nights like that. It beckoned me out of my tent to roam the sands, capturing a rare moment of peace. The desert has a split personality. Normally a harsh place, unforgiving and unbearable; yet it was still capable of winning your trust with its moments of calm, only to turn on you with its next hot breath of sand and wind. This daily unpredictability added a level of diversity that actually made the desert more interesting.

Understandably, Mother's Day was a difficult day for me. As I reflected on my mother and her unexpected passing, I missed her deeply. She was a great woman and had a profound impact on the man and the soldier I had become.

At church they had a special program about mothers, which was quite moving. Some of the men came up to me after the meeting, understanding how difficult it might have been for me, to console me and express words of comfort. Several remarked that I had been in their prayers on that day. I was touched by such thoughtfulness while in a war zone.

In the week since my return I could see that the conditions of camp life and the war were starting to wear on people. The heat, the sand, the insects, our close quarters, the lack of amenities, the lack of creature comforts, all started to affect people in different ways. As soldiers continued to wait in this harsh environment for their assignments, their true self usually crept to the surface. Some spoke about suicide, others would just as soon kill someone else that was getting on their nerves. Some just couldn't stand it anymore and didn't know what to do; others got depressed or frustrated.

The conditions were grinding away, taking some people to the limits of their tolerance. We all had our breaking points, some reaching theirs sooner than others. We had to watch each other, being aware of the signs that might appear when someone starts down that road. There were a few people to whom I paid particular attention, just to make sure I kept them moving along in a positive direction so that they would get home in one piece mentally.

Some people shut down, making it difficult to know what was really going on inside. Others were closed to begin with and would not open up to discuss their feelings. Those of us who maintained a strong healthy outlook were fluid; we accepted our circumstances and embraced changes, whatever they might be. I was fortunate not to be too affected by most of what was going on around me, making the best of the situation; there really was nothing else I could do. I refused to get too worked up about things over which I had no control.

I focused on our mission, our purpose for being there in the first place. Our challenge in Iraq was to help free a people from a dictator and assist them in setting up a new government with a bunch of untested people—people without a strong democratic tradition. We wanted them to get off on the right foot now that Saddam was gone. We knew there were many different groups and factions, all with competing and conflicting interests. Everyone there seemed to have their own agenda, with an overriding desire to protect their own domain. We knew forging freedom in that environment would be difficult. But the magnitude of that mission enabled me and many other great soldiers to keep their head in the game.

The order finally came and was an answer to prayer. I was finally moving into Iraq to work directly with Iraqi POWs at Camp Bucca in the south near the port city of Umm Qasr. I had been biding my time, trying to make the most of things in Kuwait; but there was an inner burning to move to my next station, closer to the action. I was sure there was a reason for my extended stay at Camp Udairi; it was a stepping stone preparing me for my next assignment.

Camp Bucca was a POW camp set up on a large plot of land which would be the temporary home for several thousand Iraqi prisoners. The piece of property was virtually unused by the Iraqis before the war, except for the radio station and tower that sat right in the middle of it. I expected to be there until my mission was over and all the POWs were sent back home, a process which had already begun when I arrived. Once the information they had was exploited, or if we determined they didn't have any real intelligence value, they were sent on their way. Those of higher rank or position in Saddam's regime, including 14 Iraqi generals, were still on site and were continually being questioned for information.

I had been out driving beyond the boundaries of our base a few times and had been able to see the Iraqis living in the area. Overall, the response from the locals was very positive. No matter where I went, there were crowds of kids out on the streets waiting for an American to drive by, in hopes that they would be able to catch our

Local residents come out to greet the troops with a "thumbs up."

attention. The kids stood patiently waiting on the side of road enduring the heat of the day. As they saw us coming from a distance they
begin waving. As we got closer they held up the peace sign or gave us
a thumbs up with a big smile on their face. They yelled out English
phrases, some obviously picked up from other passing troops, like
"I love you" or "Give me water." There were also some older people,
perhaps the children's parents, that had come out to wave to any
U.S. military personnel. Cars full of Iraqis would drive by, honk their
horns, and wave.

The military had to be careful, especially with the kids that hung
out on the sides of the roads. They would stand in the middle of the
road, even lying down at times, in an effort to get us to stop. They
usually sent out the smallest cutest kid so that they could encircle
the vehicle trying to steal things from inside. The bigger kids usually went right for open windows or any doors that weren't locked
and then just started grabbing stuff. Their actions seemed prompted
more by curiosity and childlike playfulness than out of any malicious
intent; still their actions posed a risk to them and to us. Despite the
warm welcome, in the back of my mind there was a lingering concern that those who might want to hurt us could appear at any time,
even in what appeared to be a welcoming throng.

Camp Bucca was named in honor of Fire Marshall Ronald Paul
Bucca, who died on September 11, 2001, during the terrorist attacks
on the World Trade Center in New York City. Radio transmissions
revealed he had ascended to the 78th floor of one of the buildings
and was putting water on a fire when he died. His body was found
close to one of the stairwells on October 23, 2001. In addition to
being a 23-year veteran of the Fire Department of New York, Ronald
Bucca was also a 29-year veteran of the military and held the rank

Antenna for Saddam's propaganda radio station in the center of Camp Bucca.

of warrant officer in the U.S. Army Reserve. Most of his career was with the 11th Special Forces Group and the Defense Intelligence Agency as an intelligence analyst.

Camp Bucca in its prior life was a propaganda radio station for Saddam Hussein. The huge radio antenna positioned in the center of the compound reached high into the clear Iraqi sky. Local villagers told us of the types of things that were broadcast during Saddam's reign, which included deliberate misinformation on the progress of Coalition troops during the early days of the war. Major Price and I occupied the radio station buildings, set up our office and operation center, and made this our home.

In an effort to make it seem more homelike, I set up our clotheslines, laid out the prayer rugs, and neatly arranged our boxes around the room. But during the intense heat of mid-afternoon, which hovered around 120° F, our office was like an oven inside. The temperatures inside the tents were no better, easily climbing to 125° F. To escape the heat, several of us slept on the roof. Every night we climbed a ladder, bedding in hand, to sleep under the stars, where a cooling breeze made conditions a little more bearable and sleep a little more possible. There were six of us sleeping on the roof, while the rest were sleeping in the tents set up not too far away. Occasionally, when the wind picked up you could see our silhouettes scampering around, grabbing our stuff, and heading down the ladder to get out of the storm.

Improvised rooftop barracks at Camp Bucca.

We had made a large cooler with pieces of Styrofoam found lying around. This makeshift ice chest was about three feet square and appropriately named the Mother of All Coolers. Amazingly, it really worked. Bags of ice could be kept in there for days. I thought that my next project would be to build the "cooler coffin," big enough to sleep in. That would have been the perfect camp bed, sleeping in a cooler on ice.

At its peak in May, there were over 10,000 prisoners at Camp Bucca, which was an unbelievable sight and an indescribable stench. It's difficult to comprehend the mess that many people can create. In addition to the prisoners, there were thousands of U.S. forces living in cramped quarters, with all of us using nothing more than a slit trench for a bathroom. Even after the prisoner population was reduced to about 1,000, there was still a stench about that place I will never forget.

Flies quickly became a serious problem. Millions of these pesky little insects would feast in the slit trenches and then zoom straight for our faces and food. They were carrying bacteria that if touched would make anyone sick. We named it the Bucca Bug, which sent many of our best soldiers running to the nearest outhouse. Miraculously, I did not get sick even once, being extremely cautious about what I touched and always keeping my hands sanitized and away from my mouth.

Through various media channels I continued to hear reports of accusations of prisoner ill-treatment by American soldiers. Self-serving human rights activists took every opportunity to cry foul play as they looked for any excuse to condemn our methods of handling prisoners. We were accused of making them live in tents in extreme temperatures, forcing them to eat substandard food, and making them endure sandstorms, snakes, scorpions, and crowded quarters. Welcome to Iraq. Where did they think all the U.S. military were living? American soldiers were surviving under the same conditions, side-by-side with the prisoners, and no one was lamenting our conditions.

The military went to great lengths to care for these prisoners of war. Upon arrival they were deloused and cleaned up. The prisoners were given new sky blue jumpsuits to wear, food they liked to eat, and any necessary medical treatment.

Outside of a few harsh words or a push of an unruly prisoner by the guards, our team of interrogators treated the prisoners appropriately, as we were trained to do. We were committed to honoring the rules established in the Geneva Convention. I never witnessed torture being used as a means to get someone to talk. Except for a few, the prisoners we dealt with were very willing to cooperate with us, the majority having surrendered right at the beginning of the war.

I had been an interrogator for 34 years and had received extensive training in the advanced art of interrogation, learning how to use the most effective psychological approaches to break an individual and obtain vital information quickly. The tactics used by military interrogators are very different from the brutal, strong-arm tactics often portrayed by Hollywood and assumed by the media. I am sure there are interrogators that worked outside of the military guidelines. But all of the interrogators I worked with operated professionally, with clear understanding of what constituted appropriate conduct and in absolute adherence to that standard.

My assignment at Camp Bucca was to work with a select group of high-ranking Iraqi officers. Each night after finishing my regular duties, a small group of us went out to the Hoover 7 Prisoner Compound to sit and talk with a most auspicious group of POWs, a group which included 14 Iraqi generals.

The setting was simple. We waited until 8 PM, when it was getting dark and cooling down a bit. A small tarp was placed on the ground in the middle of the compound, where I sat with three or four other interrogators, surrounded by 30 or 40 Iraqi prisoners sitting cross-legged in the sand.

Most of them had done what was suggested in leaflets that were air-dropped prior to the war. They surrendered during the opening days of the war and had been POWs ever since. In most cases, they laid down their weapons without firing a shot, turned over their equipment and bases, instructed their men to return to their homes, and drove out to meet our oncoming forces.

There were over 11,000 Brigadier Generals or above in the Iraqi Army (compared to 300 in the U.S. Army). Of these, only 14 actually turned themselves in to us. The really bad guys didn't surrender, but just ran back to their houses where they went into hiding. The good guys surrendered and expected they would be treated well, expedited through the process, and returned to their homes soon.

All 14 of them were mine. I had been given the assignment of interrogating these generals. They were mine to coerce or persuade, to entice or compel, and to love or hate. I began to repeatedly interrogate each one of them until every bit of information had been gleaned from them. They were now my boys. My interpreter and I would be there with them on a daily basis until I knew everything there was to know about them.

We determined, at least with this group, whose situation and condition of capture was quite different, that the best way to extract accurate intelligence was to build a certain degree of trust and confidence with them. As the relationship developed, they began to share valuable bits and pieces of information. Consequently, the interrogation strategy evolved into more of a friendly approach with these men, as we built rapport, mutual respect, and trust.

Frankly, I was impressed with the caliber of these men. For the most part they seemed to be good men, with good intentions, who were anxious to get back to their families and to assist in the process of rebuilding their country. Several of the officers spoke English quite well and most of the rest spoke enough English to get by in a limited fashion. I became close to a few of them as I spoke with them during my evening meetings, night after night.

As the prisoners gathered round us in a circle, we discussed a wide range of topics in great detail: their fate, what was expected of them, how they could help us, and what it would take before they could be released. We asked them questions, followed up on new leads, and confirmed their stories.

As a rule of thumb, whenever we went out to Hoover 7, we would take cold drinks. It probably meant more to us than it did to them, given the fact that they lived their lives without cold drinks anyway. They always enjoyed it when we brought along a snack like flatbread and hummus.

These important prisoners were surprisingly humble about their circumstances. Their greatest concern was to find out anything about the status of their families. We sincerely wanted to make their lives a little more bearable and were earnest in our desire to help them get released and home to their loved ones.

We worked with the Red Cross to get in touch with their families to alleviate any worry these officers might have. Some of them, who surrendered early in the war, were worried that Saddam, learning of their surrender, had killed their wives and children. I am also sure that many of the families imagined their beloved husbands and fathers had been killed in the fighting by the Americans. Some had as many as nine children, others had serious medical problems needing treatment, all were concerned for the welfare of their families.

After getting to know them and gaining their confidence and trust, we were successful in extracting a lot of solid intelligence from this group of generals. Others had unsuccessfully tried to get information out of them, acting as some interrogators do, being tough, cocky, heartless, and manipulative. The didn't abuse or mistreate them; they were just using the tough-guy approach. It didn't work with these well-educated and highly trained officers. I found the best way to effectively work with them was to gain their trust and then work with them from a position of sincerity and honesty.

As a result, the generals had been very cooperative, divulging information that led to a successful strike on the Fedayeen, the capturing of weapons and high-valued detainees, and other valuable intelligence. Some of their intelligence enabled us to save lives on several occasions. It was a great feeling when a piece of information would come out that was valuable, making a huge difference in what Coalition forces were able to accomplish.

One evening, I spent about three hours talking with one of the officers about aspects of Saddam's regime that he knew about. There had been so many crimes against humanity, so many illegal acts, so many war crimes, and so many corrupt activities going on in Iraq that it was sometimes difficult to know where to start.

Still they continued being held because we believed they might have additional intelligence value. Due to their high rank, we expected them to be the possessors of information relating to Saddam's vicious regime, to war crimes that had been committed, and to information that might lead to the discovery of weapons of mass destruction.

In my work around the world as a missionary, businessman, and private citizen, I have encountered individuals from all walks of life, in a variety of situations. As a soldier I have dealt with prisoners during Desert Storm, screened or interrogated hundreds of Iraqis, dealt with communist defectors, and various other people with a multitude of motivations and incentives. However, after working with these men, I became convinced that they were going to be part of the force for good in rebuilding Iraq. They are the future leaders of a free Iraq and their children will participate in the direction Iraq will take.

There were plenty of people coming forward who saw themselves as active participants in forming a new Iraq. Most were driven by personal or selfish desires, in an effort to snatch up power, position, or money in the vacuum created with Saddam's departure. We had been warned by several of the Iraqi officers, ones whose opinions we trusted, that it would be a serious mistake to allow any religious leaders to play a role in the governing of the new Iraq. One of our challenges was to identify the right people to lead the rebuilding effort.

To most of these people, freedom was a foreign concept and they were really not sure of its meaning to them collectively or individually. They were looking for direction and assistance from the U.S. military, as a bastion of freedom, to help them move toward their goals of free speech, free press, freedom to assemble, and freedom of worship. They knew they could not do this on their own; they needed the assistance of a greater stabilizing force that had their best interests in mind. I knew we all had the desire but was unsure if we knew the best possible course to make this happen. There would be mistakes made along the way. It was inevitable. At least the Iraqi officers we worked with knew of our sincere concerns about the future of their country and that we would do our best to insure their success.

On two consecutive evenings I interviewed General Hakim, a high-ranking general in the Iraqi Air Force. I spent about three hours each night going over information and questioning him in great detail. He was beyond cooperative. His demeanor was kind and gentle, his conduct was respectful and polite. He was never annoyed by the constant probing, being ever so patient and considerate. It was time well spent and generally very productive. It wasn't that the information I was able to extract was so earth shattering, but a bond was created and a relationship developed.

I took another interrogator, a 27-year old soldier, as my note-taker and a middle-aged Iraqi woman from the U.S., as my interpreter. The four of us sat on makeshift chairs or in the sand inside a small military tent, usually occupied by the MPs. I walked General Hakim through his story from the beginning, attempting to extract each and every detail. I pursued every lead, every inkling of intelligence, until I exhausted each diversion or branch of information, which then usually led me down a variety of other courses and directions. It was a painstakingly exhaustive process, but methodical and systematic.

When the military questioning was over, we began talking about our families. General Hakim became quite emotional as he started to speak of his wife and children, not knowing if they were still alive. He said he didn't mind staying at the POW camp as long as he was needed, but he just wanted some kind of assurance that his family was alive and well. He invited us to visit when the war was over and he was back home with his family, perhaps before we left to go back to the States. General Hakim was sincere about helping us in any way he could. He was intent on giving us anything he could that might be of value to us.

As we walked him back into the cage where all the other officers were kept, we had an opportunity to sit for a moment with the other generals. Each of us sat on a water jug as a chair, with the other generals standing around us. We spoke of God, the purpose of life, and the importance of having faith in God. They wondered out loud if God was punishing them for something they had done in the past. I suddenly saw them in a different light as we shared these deep personal feelings about our relationship with God.

I told them that I was a better person for having met them and that my life would never be the same after having so many meaningful experiences with them. They agreed by nodding their heads and in unison expressed their appreciation for what my team had done for them. I found tears in my eyes as I heard their words. I said to myself, "These are my brothers."

As we said our goodbyes and walked back to our Humvee, my young note-taker expressed his emotions in just a few simple words. He said he had been trying to figure out why he had come to Iraq and tonight he had found the answer. He was anxious to get home to proclaim his newfound appreciation for people, for freedom, and for the blessings he had taken for granted.

Even our interpreter commented on the special spirit that was felt and how touched she was by the whole experience. She commented on how proud her father would have been. When he was alive, he had been arrested and tortured by Saddam on three different occasions. We all walked away feeling we had just had one of those rare life experiences. There was a spiritual kinship in our midst that was felt by everyone.

One day, as I was driving around with Major Price, we decided to see if we couldn't do something good for someone. As we were contemplating the possibilities, we noticed a soldier walking along the side of the road who looked like he could use a lift. We paused and asked him if he needed a ride; he smiled and jumped right in.

As we were making small talk with him, I told him, "Today is your lucky day, because you had the good fortune of getting in the Good Luck Genie's Hummer." We had just been to the PX and I had an ice-cold pudding for him. I had just received a package from my work with the latest *Sports Illustrated* Swimsuit Edition, which I was willing to part with, reluctantly. We decided that one of the best ways to bring happiness to ourselves was to do kind things for others. We surely made a difference in that soldier's day. This action was the start of the "Good Luck Genie Campaign."

Major Price at home in Camp Bucca.

Major Price, who had become my cohort in this venture, decided to visit one of the Iraqi families that the base had taken in for assistance and refuge. The family we picked had five children, all under the age of nine. One of their daughters had a brain tumor and seemed to be mentally handicapped. We took over some cold water, cookies, candy, and a box of crackers. They were so excited to see us drop in with all the goodies. We sat for a moment and spoke to them, not with words, but with caring. They could sense our love for their little children. This family had been decimated by Saddam's brutal regime. They only knew a few words in English and I knew just a few words in Arabic. But it didn't matter, we connected with them. As our eyes met, we shared a joyful moment that transcended language.

In a small way we were playing a part in a much larger plan. The little things we did made a difference, although it wasn't apparent at first. Great things do come about by small means. It was difficult to say what affect our acts of kindness might have in the long run. Who knew what lasting impression might be made on the future leaders of this country.

Every day, when things slowed down in the afternoon, Major Price and I put on our wings and transformed ourselves into the Good Luck Genies. We rode around deliberately doing good things for other people we saw. Whether we were delivering treats, giving rides or telling jokes, we were successful in spreading some cheer.

We drove to the small town of Umm Qasr that was close by, to check on the situation of the local populace. There were many kids out on the streets hoping to see an American drive by, so they could wave, say hello, and stand close enough to the road to slap our out-stretched hands as we drove by (which sometimes really hurt!). They had been neglected for decades by a country pumping its wealth to fuel an oppressive government, a bloated military, and to line the pockets of its corrupt leaders. Little had been spent on even the most basic needs of these people.

For the most part, the people lived in mud huts—adobe brick homes with no amenities. There appeared to be no infrastructure, no public systems, no industry of any kind, and very few shops or stores. The town of Umm Qasr didn't even have its own water supply. The water had to be trucked in from other areas to be distributed at water points by large tankers. As we drove around the streets, mothers and children lined the sides, asking for even the remaining portion of the water bottles we carried around in our vehicles.

There was so much we wanted to do for these people, just to help them get their city up and running. We would have started by helping them to develop a water source for their town. As a group of citizen soldiers, we had many skills that we could have shared with them from our experiences in life back home: construction, engineering, business, manufacturing, and farming. The possibilities were limitless.

There was so much we wanted to do to win the hearts and minds of these people just by caring enough to share, to teach, and to make their lives better.

We continued to interrogate the high-ranking Iraqi officers to see what information might be extracted before we released them. We continued to take them apples, oranges or other little things to cheer them up. They had also been asking for such things as fingernail clippers, lotion, and a radio, so they could listen to the news. All these items were becoming a little harder to come by.

The Red Cross had really let these men down; they had promised to get in touch with each of their families and to bring back word of their status. Each of the prisoners had sent out three letters, requesting some kind of a response from their families, but nothing had come in return. They were understandably disturbed by the inability of the Red Cross to do much for them. After having made a lot of promises, even though their intentions had been good, the Red Cross just hadn't followed through. Their frustration was quite evident one night when the Red Cross showed up and all the prisoners refused to talk to them. The Red Cross knew they had better come back next time with some answers and some letters from their families. Some of the men even lived quite close, in Basra, which was only an hour away.

At one of our nightly meetings, I noticed that our POWs were particularly down and discouraged. A certain dark cloud hung over the camp. You could see it in their eyes, their heads hanging down; many of the men would approach us only to shake their heads and walk away. Detention, coupled with the uncertainty about the well-being of their families, started to take its toll on the men. Their continued POW status was aggravating and painful for all of us.

I sat with my team of interrogators and the generals on benches they had built out of tent poles and tent stakes. That night felt different. There was a thick silence, as if we were at a funeral, waiting for the casket to pass by. They had no words to express the feelings in their hearts. I had no words for them. Words said in the past—words of encouragement, praise, suggestions—were replaced with silence. We sat there looking into each others' eyes and after a few minutes, I felt it was time to go. As I departed several of them said, "Having you come out to see us is enough. It shows us that you haven't forgotten about us." Deep inside they worried we might forget them. Without words, just showing up that evening let them know that another soldier cared about them.

Chapter Five

Hoover 7

Good morning Iraq.

As we approached the end of May, a month had passed since President Bush declared an end to major combat operations. It had also been a month of sweltering heat and of uninterrupted sweating. Every pore in my body was a continuously leaking faucet. From the minute I woke up in the morning until I laid down at night, my clothes were soaked with sweat. We ended up drinking about six or seven 2-liter bottles of water every day—about three gallons. Fortunately, the mess hall was equipped with air conditioning so at least while we were eating we could cool down.

The lizards owned our room, but we were waging a successful war on the snakes and scorpions which filled the camp. We made a small dent in the mouse population, killing three in one day with the traps we set out. Peanut butter was the bait of choice.

The war had shifted to a guerrilla-type campaign by an organized Iraqi insurgency. Suicide bombings, sniper attacks, and ambush attacks on checkpoints and convoys became an increasing threat.

The war of good and evil went on day after day. The very worst of this society in all of its appetites, greed, and lust, was still fighting against the goodness that was trying to emerge after being suppressed for so long. Evil barely skipped a beat, transforming itself into another form or figure in order to continue the fight against the good. Iraq was becoming a vacuum and villany filled that vacuum quickly, not waiting around for the good forces that take time to form in a democratic society. Organized crime took over the minute Baghdad fell. There were still plenty of miscreants that had malevolent plans for Iraq and had begun to fill the void left with Saddam's disappearance.

The bad guys were hanging around, like circling vultures waiting for the right opportunity to pounce on their prey to regain some of their previous power or position. We needed the help of the good Iraqi people to identify who those vultures were. But there was still a significant amount of loyalty (and fear), even among the good people who professed their allegiance to us. At the same time they were not willing to rat on these bad apples who were often members of their own family tribe.

As a result, the way I approached the questioning of the prisoners was changing. I was more concerned about how we were going to shake out all the riff-raff, those who had proven through their past actions that they were only interested in taking from the Iraqi people.

I interviewed several people, all of whom proclaimed their allegiance to us, but continued to say they knew nothing, saw nothing, heard nothing, to the point of being totally ludicrous. Did they really think I was that stupid? They must have thought that if they said "I don't know" enough, they would get a bus ticket home.

We were never alone while interrogating a prisoner. We had at least one guard in the room or tent at all times. We were usually in sight or hearing distance from other guards also. We had our interpreter with us at all times and we usually had a few members of the Red Cross hanging around to observe what was going on.

We followed the Geneva Convention to a T, fully aware of our obligations, limitations, and the parameters of the interrogation process. I have witnessed or participated in hundreds of interrogations over the years and have never seen any wrongdoing that would be in violation of the rules of engagement. But interrogators are not soft.

I had to get rather tough with one of the generals who was being obstinate. Although I didn't touch him, he began crying when I started talking about his family.

With another, I was just not buying his story and told him that he'd better start coming up with the right answers. So much went on in this small country over the last 25 years under the heavy hand of a ruthless dictator. There had been so many years of relentless oppression and mistreatment that the people were still not quite sure what might happen if they started talking. I could see the fear in their eyes. I could see what being controlled for so long had done to their ability to step out of the fear box and openly betray Saddam Hussein.

In talking with a group of prisoners, I became upset with the answers I was getting. "Why should I care enough to come to Hoover 7 to help you, if you don't care enough to help yourselves? If you don't care, then maybe I should just pack up, go home, and leave you to live in this cesspool you've created."

After I got down off my soapbox, I pulled the so-called mayor of the camp aside and told him I was not happy with the answers they had been giving and let him know that people needed to start talking and giving me the straight scoop on what had been going on. I wanted answers and I'd better start getting them soon. He immediately told me the names of some people in the camp that were suspect and capable of providing me with more information.

I had so many tools of leverage at my fingertips to use when necessary to bring about the desired result. The prisoners understood that I controlled their fate and determined the extent of their stay there. They were accustomed to force and torture from the former regime, so it threw them off-guard when we used non-physical interrogation tools.

It was almost dusk as I slumped in a chair in my room, if you could call it a room. It was actually more like a cell block. It was a section of the bombed-out radio station that could be seen from anywhere in camp.

I sat there pensively with a candle from home flickering on my table. I could smell the sweet fragrance of cookies and spice which was almost able to overcome the stomach-churning smells of the camp.

Fly strips hung around the room in an attempt to put a dent in the fly population. These flies were unusually aggressive, swarming around my head and face whenever I was trying to get something done. Lizards would often dash across the floor, hoping to get lucky by snatching one of the low-flying pests.

A brave mother bird built a nest snuggled securely in some of the broken bricks and rebar in our room. For the first time, I heard the soft chirps of the chicks that must have hatched during the night. Somehow, the sound of the new life made the setting less harsh. I wondered what kind of birds they were, but before I could peek into their nest to find out, they were gone.

The uncomfortable hot nighttime temperature was a constant battle for me; without sufficient rest, I would be useless the next day. I had a small fan blowing the sultry air around the room, which at least evaporated some of the sweat that stained my shirt. It was a standard issue brown t-shirt that looked like it had been tie-dyed; the design was created by the swirls of salt stains from a day of non-stop sweating. The wind, which howled like a furnace in a foundry and felt hot enough to melt steel, finally died down making it possible to drift off to sleep—slumber that was much needed and appreciated.

There were many types of conflict going on in Iraq simultaneously: Conflict with each other, conflict with the system, conflict with our enemy, conflict with our own weaknesses, conflict with the environment, and conflict with temptations. Every conflict forces you to take a side.

As we tried to make sense of the conflicts that surrounded us, I received a report of a statement made by an Iraqi medical doctor to one of our colonels. His words were touching and provided a much needed pat on the back for all of us.

> Colonel, I want to express how I feel in my heart and if you can, I ask that you pass my words to your leaders and commanders and the marines and soldiers who suffered and are suffering for my country. I want all of you to know that the great majority of Iraqis applaud your coming, your success in battle, and your efforts to be kind, decent people.

> We suffered for many years and no one would help us— not even our Arab brothers. Only America had the strength, not only in military power, but also in vision, in character, in moral authority, in love for its fellowmen to come to our aid. I know it is hard for the soldiers now, they have no air-conditioning in their vehicles, they must live on our streets to protect us, and they are away from their families. I want them to know that we know the sacrifices they make for us. I pray to Allah that they will sacrifice no more: too many already have sacrificed so much.

> I also want to apologize for some of our young people who are not mature enough to understand what you have done and what you have given us. We have not known freedom for a long time, so it will take time to truly appreciate what a glorious gift you have given us.

> Many of us blame the sanctions for all our problems. It was not the sanctions that created what we see today, it was

the regime that existed everywhere, including this building that I work in, the Ministry of Health. It was the regime that cheated the people out of what was rightfully theirs by God's laws.

When I talk with my family and friends, I tell them that what is going on now, with the shortages and suffering, is like a surgery for cancer. Saddam was a cancer. When one operates for a cancerous tumor, one must cut through the muscle and sometimes the bone, to get the entire tumor out. After the tumor is removed, the patient's muscles and bones hurt greatly, and the pain continues while healing. Over time, the patient sees a change, the patient begins feeling and doing better.

That is how it is in Iraq. The Americans came and took out the awful cancer and now we must work through the pain of recovery, but eventually we will enjoy a full life, free of pain, with no fear of cancer. I want to thank all of you from the bottom of my heart.

The doctor's remarks were not uncommon, but they didn't speak loudly enough for the media to hear. It was always the other side in Iraq that made the news, the side that was not the majority, but was the outspoken dark side, the over-zealous, fanatical fundamentalist minority who would rather stir up the pot than try to make the pot better. There are those who profess to be religious but are full of hatred and greed. Evil has many disguises in this part of the world and too often comes as a wolf in sheep's clothing.

The MPs took over one of our buildings next to the radio station, displacing some of our soldiers back to the living area where most of the tents were. They had a few mentally disturbed prisoners who needed

Prisoner compound at Camp Bucca.

to be placed in a hard facility where they could not commit bodily harm to themselves or others.

Cells were built in the open area of this building and barbed wire was placed around it, with a sign over the front door calling it "Iraqatraz." The army built up dirt berms around the camp and alongside the roads inside the camp. It looked like some giant mole had been digging tunnels. For security, the berms were topped with razor wire. In addition to its obvious protective placement, the razor wire also managed to catch any litter that blew across the compound or from anywhere else in Iraq, for that matter. The litter-decorated berms added a festively tacky atmosphere to a pretty bleak setting. It was always amusing to see what the fence would catch next.

Each night I climbed the ladder, pillow and poncho in hand, to reach my resting spot. The addition of floodlights lit up the whole area, including the roof of my building, making it more difficult to sleep at night. The small mattress I slept on resembled a baby crib mattress, only a little longer. There was a constant layering of sand that piled up on my mattress and around the roof throughout the day. I could only imagine how much sand I inhaled daily. I was surprised I didn't cough up mudballs from the depths of my lungs.

The prisoners had been worried about the increase of scorpions and snakes infiltrating their area. Every time we went out to Hoover 7 they let us know how many they had seen or killed, in an effort to convince us to give them cots to sleep on and elevate them from the ground. We empathized and were soon able to get some cots for them. Seeing the jubilation in their faces when the cots arrived was like watching a child opening Christmas presents.

I continued working in the fenced area of Hoover 7 where the generals were being held. After a number of days, a greeting ritual was established that transcended our native language and cultural barriers. I would meet with them in their tent, often sitting on the floor with them. As I entered, I would address each man by name and look him straight in the eye. I would say a few Arabic words of greeting and ask him how he was doing. After shaking his hand, I would put my hand on my heart as each of them did likewise, implying that we are brothers and that we understood each other's heart.

In the evening after supper, we went out to the pens for our nightly screenings and interrogations with the generals, who were now like our own children. As a team, we felt a great deal of responsibility for their well-being. It was as if they were our flock of sheep, gathering around whenever we ventured out to see how they were doing.

I returned one night from Hoover 7 quite late, around 11 PM. Going out to the cage and seeing the depressed state the men were in took a lot out of me. We had a nice talk though, informing them that we would write a letter to President Bush to see if we could force a decision out of someone. It was as if we were punishing them for doing exactly what we had asked them to do. They had read our leaflets, which asked them to lay down their arms and surrender. In exchange, we would take care of them. They did as we asked, then we threw them into prison, where they had been for 72 days. Once we were finished interrogating them, the generals were more valuable to American interests as free men capable of building a free Iraq than as prisoners of war.

As we received our daily ice delivery, I made sure we had an extra bag to take out to the prisoners, so they could at least enjoy a cold drink once in a while. I was working with Major Garrity who seemed to be on the same wavelength, intent on doing the right thing by these men. Several times we met out there at the same time with ice bags in hand, both of us making an effort to ease the discomfort of those good men.

My happiest day since arriving at Camp Bucca came on a Sunday. I was working in the office writing up some interrogation reports. My rooftop bunk buddy came running in, beckoning me to follow him quickly over to the building next door. I jumped up quickly, stopped everything I was doing, and fast-stepped it next door, not sure what all the fuss was about.

I entered the briefing room just in time to see one of the generals from Hoover 7 sitting in the room with a woman and a young man, whom I immediately realized were his wife and son. I threw my arms around them all, greeting his family with the universal language of an embrace. He and I had been close for some time, so I was glad he wanted to share that moment with me. It was marvelous to see him be reunited with his family, even briefly.

There had been no official contact with the wife and son; they just showed up at the front gate, thinking that perhaps their husband and father might be held captive inside this POW camp. He had really been down, not knowing what might have happened to them. Now everything had changed. Even though he was not going to be able to leave, at least he knew his family was safe. He had been quite a whiner, in a depressed state for some time; but he became a new man from that moment on, with a twinkle back in his eye and a ready smile.

★

Once again it was time to play Good Luck Genies. We started out by procuring a box of apples—okay, we stole them—along with a few bags of ice and some flatbread. We took them out to our officer prisoners in Hoover 7. It was worth doing just to see the looks on their faces.

On another occasion, I took Steve, a willing accomplice and member of my team, out to Hoover 7 loaded with a shovel and some Styrofoam. We proceeded to build a homemade cooler for the high-ranking officers, so their ice wouldn't melt the minute we dropped it off. We loaded their new cooler with some ice, placed some water jugs in it, put the lid on, covered it with a tarp, and told them to enjoy. I also dropped off some potatoes and onions for them to cook up as an addition to their daily dose of boring food.

Our kindness was consistently returned. One of the generals whom I had grown quite close to, an infantry commander named Matta, told me through his friend that he had a gift for me. Of course, I told him that I didn't need a gift of any sort; all I wanted was the news that they would be released. He was determined to present me with his gift. He gave me his prayer beads, with 103 beads. This took me by surprise, since I knew how much those meant to him. Prayer beads were a part of them, as a baby would hold on to a pacifier; they were forever counting and rubbing their beads. I was deeply touched by his gesture of kindness.

I wasn't expecting my birthday to be different from any other day in Camp Bucca. But while I was sitting at the computer at 6:30 AM a few of the men came in singing "Happy Birthday" and holding a plate full of cake pieces they had lifted from the mess hall the night before. There was a lonely toothpick burning on top of one of the pieces. Steve, who was my son's age, had written me a brief note, thanking me for my example and leadership. I was touched by his

The gang at Bucca.

thoughtfulness and his kind words complimenting me for all I had done.

That evening we returned to Hoover 7 for our discussions. A few of the prisoners, once they saw me, returned quickly to their respective tents, only to return moments later, with a small envelope. One of them had taken the time to actually make a ribbon out of paper from a brown sack that he taped to the top of the envelope. Someone had told them that it was my birthday. They had written a short letter wishing me the best of birthdays and long life for many more. They apologized for not being able to give me anything more, but I assured them that their friendship and thoughtful letters were more than I could have hoped for.

One of the generals gave me a small box of breath mints, which he wrapped in white lined paper. I was startled by such an expression. Mustering composure, I thanked him from the bottom of my heart for his kind gesture, putting my hand on my heart hoping that he would understand. I later read the letters when I returned to the privacy of my room, knowing I might be overcome with emotion.

I was on a journey to rediscover myself in Iraq. It was an evolution of the self through deliberate actions and abundant service. My biggest leaps forward in the process seemed to occur when I lost myself in the concerns of others.

The irony of being in Iraq on Friday the 13th did not escape us. What a great place to be on that lucky day, out in the hotter-than-hell desert sands. As the temperatures climbed into the 120s in the shade, we all decided to become somewhat nocturnal, as most of the other creatures in the desert, taking shelter in the afternoons from the blazing rays of the sun. I usually ate dinner around 5 PM and then headed out to the pens around 6 PM to work with the prisoners. I was sure that the prisoners would rather not deal with us during the peak heat of the day. We certainly didn't want to deal with them.

In talking to some of these men, I had come to understand what it took to be successful in Saddam's army. One of the officers put it quite succinctly: "If you want to be successful in the Iraqi army you need to be a donkey." In other words, you need to be as dumb as a donkey—one that sees nothing, knows nothing, hears nothing, and asks nothing.

Not all the prisoners were in good standing with us. I had a few guys whom I treated in a different manner, never to torture or mistreat, but I ran a variety of different strategies and approaches on them during the interrogation process. One such uncooperative character was a general with important governmental responsibilities, General Mahmood, or "Dark Eyes," as I called him. I was running an assortment of approaches with him to see how he might react.

Mahmood was mine, and I was committed to finding a way to make him talk. It was not easy and I was constantly praying during the interrogation that I would be inspired to know what would work next. I was humbled by the responsibility, knowing that I was going to need some special help to get this nut to crack. I was working with him on a daily basis until such time that I felt he was beginning to be truthful with me about his involvement with the old regime.

Dark Eyes was a real bad dude who had reportedly committed many crimes against fellow Iraqis. My job was to break him down to the point where he would be chirping like a bird, divulging some real hard facts, but I knew it was going to take some time. Running a strategy is all about being patient and sticking with the approach.

We knew that as a high-ranking government official, he was almost certainly involved in all kinds of illegal and corrupt activities, which included policing the officers in the military to insure they were following Saddam's wishes. It was widely known that he took part in activities involving promotions, dismissals, imprisonments, and executions. He was a pretty big fish and putting up a good fight, so I was committed to keeping him on the line for as long as it would take to reel him in.

In my attempts to break Dark Eyes, I was assisted by information provided by the other prisoners who were working with me. The generals were united against him and provided me with a wealth of information. General Hakim even wrote down a few questions he felt I should ask Mahmood.

Piece by piece, we moved closer to our goal of breaking him down to the point that he was willing to answer any question that I might ask. Interrogators are not always successful, but when you see a glimmer of light, indicating a change in attitude or a change in the level of resistance, then you get even hungrier for the kill—figuratively speaking. Sometimes it was a matter of who wears out whom. Like an animal of prey looking for one weakness to pounce on, I jumped on any vulnerability in this POW and gnawed at it.

I took away his cigarettes initially, which he struggled with, having smoked four packs a day for thirty years. I took away any comfort items. I took him out of the general populace where he was with the other officers. They actually warned me that if he was left in there he would be killed because of his involvement with Saddam's regime. I took away his blanket, forcing him to sleep in the sand. I made him distinctly aware that I was in charge of his life and everything depended on his cooperation. He knew who his daddy was. I was in total control of his life and he knew it. I was going to snap him like a crisp twig.

It was actually an exciting game of mental tug-of-war; first I would pull tightly, then I'd slowly release, only to snatch the rope up again to pull some more. I was gradually developing a relationship with him to the extent that I wanted to and to the extent that it suited my needs. I had a mission to accomplish which I intended to fulfill anyway I could within my guidelines.

I had been interrogating General Mahmood for several weeks, working him day-in and day-out to extract every ounce of intelligence. I had to play a variety of roles, at times acting totally frustrated and upset, dropping a few well-placed swear words to accentuate my feelings and to get my point across.

At times my interpreter refused to interpret what I was saying. She had a hard time dropping a few "F-bombs" on Dark Eyes. I was not quite sure what she was saying, but I sensed that she was softening up my words. Although, at times, she got emotionally immersed in the discussion dropping in a few of her own choice swear words, ones I would never use, such as references to deity.

Mahmood had been responding to her intensity and expression of anger. "Please be easy on me, sister," he would say. He really hated it when she got mad at him. So I tried to use that to my advantage as often as possible. He had numerous nervous habits revealing just how concerned he was about what the future held for him. But I knew he was not going anywhere soon and perhaps for the rest of his life.

After a few weeks in the cage, I was starting to see some progress and Dark Eyes was becoming more and more cooperative. I noticed his demeanor and attitude were changing. Over time, he seemed to be breaking down, finally giving up information we had been asking for and which we knew he had. My interpreter was also noticing the change, commenting on how his proud and arrogant attitude was beginning to crumble.

The changes we were seeing were the result of using well established, sophisticated interrogation approaches over an extended period. This is what interrogation was all about. We were running complicated psychological approaches, changing from one to another, running several at one time, and paying strict attention to the prisoner's reactions. It was the challenge of man against man, mind against mind, me against him. That is when interrogation really gets interesting. I loved being able to get creative, using all available resources to come up with a plan of attack and then watch it unfold. The design, the orchestration, and the implementation was pure fun. And when it really worked there was no greater feeling.

I have found over the years that working on building trust with a friendly approach was in most cases the most effective method. But that doesn't mean I always start out with that approach. It was a matter of learning how to read a person, which is not a precise science, but one in which I had developed a proficiency.

Being able to make a connection with someone, in a positive way, in an environment of trust and sincerity is a more productive way of working. Interrogation is much like a sales process: gaining acceptance, identifying needs, reviewing benefits and advantages, and overcoming objections. The better we were at identifying the prisoner's needs, the more effective we became.

Interrogation is a team effort and requires more than one brain to bring it all together. I was using an interpreter as part of the team, which added another difficult dimension to the process. It was extremely important that we have total confidence in our interpreter, and that we know the interpreter's limitations. Fortunately, the interpreter I used was also a trained interrogator and we each had an in-depth understanding of the other's thought processes. With this powerful synergy in place, things really started to happen.

Interpreting is a difficult task, one that requires special skills and abilities, such as being a good listener, knowing what you are hearing, reading the tone of voice, the inner meaning, sifting through contradictions, and knowing the complexities of language. Some of our interpreters were just not good listeners, which was obvious by the crazy off-base answers we got sometimes. If the subject is not hearing the question correctly, then the answer will be off. But more frequently I found that the disconnect occurred in what the interpreter thought he was hearing in the response. Since I was looking for any sign of weakness or a special need, having an interpreter who was not a good listener impaired the whole process.

It was hard to play a game of word trapping, when you didn't hear all the words, especially the way the word was used or the tone of voice in which it was said. It is painstaking work to go through a full interrogation using an interpreter, especially when you are trying to run a specific approach. The real meaning can be lost along the way, without the interrogator even knowing it, bringing about a totally different result.

Most of the interpreters were hired from companies which had a pool of interpreters, who were generally native speakers of Arabic and U.S. citizens living in the United States. I decided to give them a few lessons on military vocabulary, common phrases and sentence structure, areas in which we saw some weakness. I felt it was important to have them understand what our expectations were. I wanted to give them a test to assess their abilities, and determine areas of improvement. But they were offended when they heard the very word "test." Ultimately, no test was given.

I knew who I could use, in what situations, and with what limitations. I knew we were in trouble with some when the interpreter got some basic military words wrong or got stumped by a few words that he or she should have known. There were many times when talking to them at breakfast, I noticed that the simplest things were being missed in our conversation. They did a great job overall, but I knew they could have done better.

The noise I was hearing from the States about the naysayers and doubters attacking the United States military and the President regarding our country's actions in Iraq was appalling. These critics ignored what the world has known for years, that Saddam had chemical, biological, and nuclear weapons programs, which he was purchasing from France, Russia, and China, and also developing himself. He had used some of these weapons over the years and would not hesitate to use them again.

Everyone we spoke with in Iraq knew that Saddam had the weapons programs—even the United Nations acknowledged that. They just didn't know where the weapons were located or what happened to them. Based on my reports from interrogating the Iraqi generals, it was a well established fact that Saddam had been burying weapons for years in places all over Iraq. I personally conducted an interrogation that involved the disclosing of information relating to the burying of chemical weapons back in the mid-1990s. The U.N.

was aware of his burying practices also. But the mainstream media didn't want to run with those stories.

Saddam Hussein was all about secrecy, a whole regime built around secret organizations, secret police, and secret guards. We found several mass graves with thousands of unidentified bodies. His continuing strategy of distortion, denial, and deception prolonged the survival of his regime and diminished the stature of the United States in the eyes of the world. Much of the intelligence we collected validated President Bush's position.

The critics should have spoken with one of our prisoners, General Hakim, Iraqi Air Force commander, who tried to make the best of the time he had on his hands as a POW. He had developed a number of great ideas for the rebuilding of Iraq. He approached me one night with an envelope in his hand, which contained his well thought out plan of action in resolving a number of issues that faced Coalition forces. He felt that his surrender and detention had given him the time to develop these ideas. He commented that the other officers in the camp were all so self-consumed with the thought of getting out that, as he put it, they were totally empty-headed. Hakim was committed to using his time wisely, since he said it was God-sent.

I told him that I loved his attitude, expressing my own ideas about taking advantage of the opportunities that come our way. God tries to teach us something, but often we are so blinded by our own issues that we miss the chance to become a tool in His hands.

As the post-war season dragged on, I continued to be responsible for the high-ranking officers of Hoover 7. Since we had collected most of the intelligence they could provide, I was there to give them hope and to expedite their release. I was their advocate and their voice connecting them to the upper echelons of our command, which held the keys to their release. I was also the one who made a daily effort to extract any remaining bit of valuable information out of them. I had a mission that straddled both sides of the fence. I had a military obligation on one hand, a humanitarian mission on the other, and a determination to succeed at both.

One day the Red Cross actually came through with messages from a few of the officers' families. What a miracle! And what a load off of my shoulders to hear the good news. The prisoners were relieved to know that the families that had been reached were all safe.

After seeing an ad in the newspaper for cell phones, with a phone number for the city of Mosul, the prisoners came up with an idea. They would call that number and have whoever answered the phone either call or go directly to the prisoner's home so that family members could get on the phone. I was delighted to discover that their plan actually worked. Using this strategy they were able to hook up an Iraqi Navy general with his family. Although some prisoners were able to receive comforting news from home, they were still frustrated by their continued detention, having totally cooperated with us in every way.

In order to be released, each individual had to be interrogated and cleared by our MI unit as well as by Criminal Investigation Division (CID), who did a background check and their own interrogation of each prisoner. The approval for releasing them went up the chain, almost to the Pentagon. I was once told that the approval for their release was sitting on Rumsfeld's desk—although that was not very likely.

One evening, I carried with me a list of names of individuals who had been cleared by CID. The minute I took out the list and motioned to my interpreter to begin explaining it, the men began to swarm like bees, hovering for their chance to dive in to check for their name on the list.

Their reward started to arrive when we were actually successful in getting two of our Hoover 7 high-ranking officers released. What a feeling! After all this time, I couldn't hold back the excitement. I took a few people on our team out to Hoover 7 to share the news. It was quite a moment, seeing their reaction to the announcement. They quickly gathered their belongings then dashed out to board the homebound bus.

As the first two men walked out of Hoover 7, I was able to take part in an Iraqi tradition. Everyone picks up seven rocks, which they throw behind the person who is leaving, symbolizing in a fun-filled way, that they want the person to leave for good, never to come back. I really got into the spirit of the moment, picking up the biggest rocks I could find. I chucked seven rocks at each person, telling them to leave and never come back.

Within a few days I was able to send seven more officers to their respective homes. The news came around midnight. As I ran into the tent, I threw my arms around each of them, one by one, communicating without words our shared happiness. That was a victorious moment, to see our hard work finally pay off.

The POWs were understandably worried about their personal property that was taken when they were captured. Some of them had large sums of money, others had their car taken by Coalition forces, others just a watch or a special pen. The military worked to honor their claims, to find their belongings, or to compensate them with cash for the things that were missing. We made every effort to insure they were treated with fairness. For the most part, their requests were not questioned and were honored in good faith.

Tracking these personal effects was an enormous task. It wasn't like the Army had some sophisticated inventory handling system to insure that everything traveled with the prisoners to their final destination. Some Iraqis were captured by troops moving quickly through the area as they pushed northward. The sheer number of prisoners, along with the speed of the troop movement, made it almost impossible to keep up with all their personal effects.

As we were waiting for our seven officers to depart, I went out to get them some cigarettes, a few bottles of cold water, and some things to munch on for the long journey home. I also grabbed an interpreter so I could give them a few final words.

I told them it was time to go home and get to work—working as an active participant in the rebuilding of their nation. It was their turn to make a difference any way they could. Their new freedom had come at an immense cost, one they needed to work to pay back. I told them to not be lazy, not to just sit back and do nothing. I told them that they couldn't allow the smaller but louder minority to direct the course of their new nation.

I will never forget the look on the prisoners' faces as they contemplated their expected freedom. They were so appreciative, expressing over and over their thanks. I gave much of that credit to the diligent efforts of two U.S. Army majors who worked to assure their release. Major Garrity and Major Price had really been the driving force to make that glorious day happen.

One night, I spoke with one of the Iraqi generals in a friendly discussion about the war, the U.S. and the value of it all. We were discussing the cost of Operation Iraqi Freedom in lives and resources. I told him that there were many people back home questioning why the United States had come to this country to conduct this operation. The strength of his conviction and the passion of his response surprised me.

The general said, "As leader of the free world and as the last superpower, it is America's responsibility and duty to help the oppressed people of the world enjoy the freedom that you do—not just because it is your duty, but because you can. You have the ability, the resources, the manpower, and the will. Your very nature as free people compels you to want to provide the opportunities of a free and independent society to others. You have always shown a genuine compassion for the oppressed of the world." With just a hint of sadness, he pressed further, "If you don't, who will? Who is going to step forward to make this dream possible for us?"

One day a few truckloads of prisoners arrived, about 400 in all. Most of them were criminals from Iraqi prisons sent here until the new prison was built. These were convicted rapists, thieves, murderers, and other violent types—not quite the right customer for us. As interrogators we focused primarily on military or government personnel, or any member of an anti-Coalition organization, of which there was no shortage. Fortunately, I didn't get involved in interrogating the criminals to any great degree.

With the worst of these criminals came some violent and bizarre behavior. Some would try to kill themselves or to run away. One who tried to escape was shot. Another one tried to charge a guard with a club and he was shot also (after the guard fired four warning shots into the air). This was not a business for the faint of heart.

Several days after the arrival of the criminals, the generals from Hoover 7 were called up by CID to be questioned further, forcing a number of them to be transported and stuck in a hot tent all day waiting for interrogation. The generals were upset that they were transported and grouped with all the newly arrived criminals. They were offended and hurt to think that we would mix them with this unsavory element and treat them as if they were common criminals.

The generals were disgusted with the treatment, not being fully aware of the problems that existed, which prevented the guards from being able to segregate the prisoners. I went over and spoke with the MPs and the CID to explain the situation, hoping to be able to come up with some ideas. They were all open to feedback, actually initiating a few solutions.

I understood the generals' concern but sympathized more with the two generals who had not made a fuss about the treatment, Generals Hakim and Matta. It was interesting to see how each individual reacted to different situations, under different degrees of pressure and stress. It was like peeling back an onion, with all its layers, until you get right down to the guiding belief system of each man. As all the facades came down, one by one, I saw the unvarnished core of each individual.

Chapter Six

4th of July

They've always had a 4th of July in Iraq, but it takes Americans to really celebrate it. We decided to give our soldiers a half day off to kick back and get crazy. The gang did a variety of things to celebrate, but when it got dark I stopped the fun and games for a moment of reflection. I passed out glow sticks, gathered us in a circle, turned on Lee Greenwood's song, "God Bless the U.S.A.," and had a moment of silence as we listened to the lyrics. I gave a brief speech afterwards and spoke of my time back in 1991 when I was in the Middle East for the first time. I described how I would get choked up every time we raised the American flag and played that song. I expressed my appreciation and told them how proud I was to be serving with them.

Later I took the boom box out to Hoover 7 to play some music for the generals. I played music by Josh Groban, Charlotte Church, and some classical stuff. But they didn't really get into the spirit of the music until we played some of their Middle Eastern music by Egyptian songstress, Umm Kulthum. Once that music came on, their eyes lit up and they were transformed, as they let the music transport them back to their homes and families.

I then made my way over to the tent of General Matta, whose prayer beads I still kept. He had hurt his back lifting something and had been laid up for nearly two weeks. We had grown quite close during his internment. His bunk buddy, General Hakim, spoke English well enough for the three of us to spend significant time together. General Matta was lying prostrate on the floor, while General Hakim and I sat on the floor by his side, discussing the events of the day and plans for the future. I showed General Matta a few exercises to help his lower back, being familiar with back pain myself.

General Hakim was possibly the most unselfish person I had ever met. He once told me that he wanted to be the last person to leave the camp, just to insure that all the other generals got out. Whenever I brought out something for the group, he made sure everyone else got some before he did. He was the one person who viewed his detention as a time to prepare for building the future of Iraq.

The two men began to express some uncomfortable feelings. Because I hadn't come out to Hoover 7 for a couple of nights, the two generals feared that I had been hastily transferred from Camp Bucca without the chance to say goodbye. They told me they would always be there for me. If I were sent to downtown Baghdad they would be my shield, literally, to defend me against all would-be attackers. They looked forward to the time when I would be able to visit with them in their homes, meet their families, and partake of their hospitality. The sincerity of their words and the pure intent of their hearts touched me deeply.

I later spoke with General Mohammed, taking notes on a plan he had to secure the two roughest areas of Iraq—Fallujah and Ramadi—in order to prevent the loss of any additional American soldiers. He had at his disposal two brigades that he claimed he could call up, that would secure the areas from additional attacks against Coalition forces. As he spoke, I felt his sincerity to protect American lives, confident he would be successful in accomplishing his plan.

As I returned to my office to type up a spot report reviewing General Mohammed's plan, I ran into Major Garrity, who was responsible for the care of the prisoners. She mentioned an email she

SFC Gilson plays with some of the refugee children whose families were given a home at Camp Bucca.

had received earlier in the day from a U.S. Army major stationed near Baghdad who just happened to be looking for General Mohammed.

The U.S. Army major had sent an email to every camp in Iraq hoping to find the Iraqi general he had worked with in the initial phase of Operation Iraqi Freedom, the general who had surrendered with all his men the first day of the war without firing a shot. The major was concerned about the general's whereabouts and the reasons for his detainment. He wanted to pursue getting him released so he might work with him in the areas of most concern—the same areas I was just discussing with the general. It was exciting to see good things happening that would be the start of great things to come.

A few days later I went back out to interrogate Dark Eyes, General Mahmood. We were convinced he had corroborating evidence of some of the horrific things the regime had been involved in. I had effectively worked every angle with him, extracting large amounts of information. After a month and a half he was starting to look hammered from the experience. He fidgeted about nervously playing with a button on his clothes while tapping his foot incessantly, all the while sweat pouring down his forehead. There was no inner light to be found in his dark empty eyes, only selfishness and evil. There was such a contrast between him and General Hakim. This only further confirmed my opinion that we needed to find the right men to lead this nation; there were plenty of the wrong ones still lurking around.

In the searing heat of summer, my fan only pushed the hot air around the room faster, further dehydrating my skin and mouth. I ventured out into the sun to recover a bottle of cold water from our home-made cooler. The wind coming off the desert burned my face with the same feeling you get sitting too close to a fire. The hot dry air burned my lungs with every breath. My only escape from this punishment was my twice-daily entrance to the dining facility to partake of the refrigerated air while I ate.

Then came a high-caliber sandstorm, the likes of which I hadn't seen for some time. I found my refuge in the old bombed-out radio station. We had spent much time securing every crack and crevice, to make this old building as sandproof as possible. I had covered up every hole, every opening, and every window. Despite our sand-proofing efforts, the demon granules crept through into my inner sanctuary laying down a fine coat of sand on everything around me. It was coming in no matter what.

The wind outside was screaming, demanding to enter my place of refuge, to dump its load on everything in sight. I was covered with many layers of fine silt, changing the color of my skin as if I worked inside some kind of a milling operation. Even though it was not visible to the naked eye, one swipe of my hand across my brow revealed coarseness to the touch confirming the sand's presence. My computer needed constant care to keep the sand from clogging up its systems.

Walking outside into the fierceness of the sandstorm, I could feel my bare skin being hit by millions of microscopic BBs. Even with goggles, my vision was impaired, not being able to see more than a few feet ahead. It was a total sand blackout with tents, equipment, and vehicles all disappearing behind a khaki cloak of wind and sand, making it almost impossible to breathe.

I had been alerted through an email that some Army brass from Camp Doha were planning on coming up to ask the generals in Hoover 7 a few questions. I had many such requests and consequently didn't pay much attention to it. I prepared the usual packets of information for ten of the Iraqi generals I had chosen to be interviewed. I provided an overview of the circumstances of their capture, their level of knowledge, and my recommendations. I prepared one of the tents out at Hoover 7 with a few chairs to accommodate the people who were expected to show up. I didn't quite know what to expect. I had not been told what type of prisoner they were interested in, what type of questions would be asked, or the intent of the meeting.

The convoy arrived in two large SUVs, with seven people, a variety of ranks below the rank of general were represented. We made our introductions, reviewed our plans for the day, gained their acceptance, and proceeded with the itinerary.

We loaded the visiting dignitaries back into their vehicles, with Major Price, an interpreter, and me leading the way in our vehicle. We passed through the first checkpoint to enter the compound and proceeded to Hoover 7. As we entered the gate and moved across the sand towards the tent, the fierceness of the wind caused us to walk back and forth in a zigzagging fashion.

The prisoners were huddled in their tents to escape the wind, awaiting our arrival. As we entered the camp, the designated leader of the prisoners, General Shamil from the Iraqi Navy, came out to greet the group. I gave him the list of those we wanted to talk to, stepping quickly towards the tent to get out of the sandstorm. We had previously instructed the prisoners to come into the tent one by one in the order on the list.

As arranged, the prisoners came in and sat down in front of the highest ranking visitor while the others, in chairs or on the floor, were gathered around to either listen or to participate in the discussion. Notepads were out, the tape recorder turned on, and pens were in hand as the prisoners entered the tent.

One by one, the questions were asked and the answers were given. The questions were simple, direct, and to the point. The prisoners answered completely and succinctly according to their level of knowledge. But something unexpected began to materialize. There was a warm, peaceful spirit in the room. The interviewers got their answers, but they felt much more. They looked into the eyes of each of these men. They heard the generals' honest and sincere answers, filled with hope and optimism, which spoke volumes to everyone sitting in the circle.

Our American military officials witnessed the future of Iraq streaming in before them. They gained a vision of what could be done and what needed to be done. I saw the lights go on as they caught the vision of the possibilities. They saw the solution sitting right before them.

The visiting officers heard the generals describe their plight, their heroic efforts, their bright plans for the future, and their willingness to play an active role in building a democratic Iraq. But more than what they heard, our visitors were impressed by what they felt.

One U.S. officer was so touched that he slipped $40 in my pocket requesting that I buy something for the generals. Many commented that these were the men that would rebuild Iraq, taking key positions throughout the country to lead this nation into a new era.

It was like creating a cake, with each prisoner we laid down another layer. General Hakim was the icing, and General Matta, was the cherry on top. I couldn't have picked a better lineup for the visitors to meet.

After each prisoner finished their battery of questioning, I would rise and walk them to the door of the tent. They would whisper to me in their broken English, "Good? Did I do good?" It was funny that they would look to me to provide some confirmation regarding their performance.

When the meetings were over, the U.S. officers all recommitted themselves to fighting for the freedom of these generals and to seek their partnership in this rebuilding process. They complimented us on our efforts in developing strong personal relationships with each of the officers.

As their convoy of SUVs drove away from sight, Major Price and I gave an exuberant high five to each other in an expression of satisfaction, "Finally someone gets it. Someone else has caught the vision of what this is all about." We were so pumped up with the hope that someone else at a higher level, with more clout than either of us, had seen the light.

That night I returned to Hoover 7 to see how the boys were doing. I was totally taken back by their enthusiasm and hope for a positive outcome of this experience. I reaffirmed my confidence in them and let them know they would do many great things for Iraq.

We all had hope for a rebirth of this land and to find a course that would realize the potential of Iraq. What once was the cradle of civilization was now a land lost in time, its potential anesthetized by Saddam's numbing and deadening regime.

★

As soon as I answered the phone I knew it was trouble. The guards at the front checkpoint informed me that there was a bunch of upset family members wanting to visit their loved ones. Normally, we allowed family visits on Thursdays, Fridays, and Saturdays. But this week, due to an increase in the threat level and the lack of MP support, all visitations were canceled. But nobody bothered to tell the families.

Many of these family members had driven halfway across the country to visit their loved ones, only to find out that all visitations were canceled for the week. Many of them had spent their last bit of money just to pay for the round-trip taxi ride.

Someone had to diffuse the situation. I went out with an interpreter to try to explain the situation to some very disappointed people. I felt badly but was forced to comply with the camp commander's decision. I offered to take the bags of food they had brought for their family members and any messages they might have. It was an unfortunate situation, one that really pulled on my heartstrings. I was usually a very accommodating person, willing to do what ever was needed to resolve a situation, but in this case my hands were tied.

Those were tough times for all, not just for the prisoners. All of us were away from our homes and families and had to face our own sacrifice and suffering. There were young men who had married right before they were mobilized, others who had a wife and small children, some who left a pregnant wife and missed the birth of their first child. Additionally, there were many with financial crises or had been called upon to interrupt their education. All of us were missing life back home.

Once regular visits were reinstated, a crowd started forming at the front gate early in the morning, much earlier than was required. I was not sure why they felt they had to get there so early. It was not like one family was going to get ahead of another or get to see their loved one longer than another. The crowd was generally unruly, one family trying to get in front of another, jockeying for position to see who was going to get on the bus first. The funny thing was that they all got on the bus at the same time.

I always went out to meet the families of the generals to insure they got on the bus without any glitches and to pick up any bags of food or supplies they might have brought. With the general's POW numbers in hand, I went through the crowd trying to identify those families with appointments to see one of the generals hoping that I might make first contact with them. I tried to put their minds at ease, assuring them their loved ones were doing well.

By the time I was finished with the generals' families my Hummer looked like a Meals on Wheels van—full of assorted bags, food, small suitcases, watermelons, and dates. Everybody brought dates. One of the families brought me a huge bag of dates to personally consume. I love dates—but not ten pounds of them. I gathered up

Prisoners' families at the Camp Bucca gate.

bed sheets, pajamas, cakes, and huge containers of rice, all for the prisoners.

When I went out to the front gate, I saw the wife of one of the generals whom I had met before. She wasn't on my list of those who had appointments, but even so I felt inclined to assist her in visiting her husband. After making a deal with the MPs I arranged for her to get on the bus which would take her inside the camp, while I dashed over to Hoover 7 to pick up her husband.

The bus arrived at the visiting location prior to my departure for Hoover 7. When she saw me, she immediately demanded to know where her husband was, unappreciative of the big favor I was doing and unaware that I was working way outside of the box for her.

When I went to pick up her husband, he had a huge suitcase full of items he had received from the MPs: cookies, cheese, toiletries, paper items, etc. I was concerned that he was abusing the system, asking for items from the guards then saving them all for his family. I knew his intentions and concerns for his family were good and that his family could probably use the items, but whatever he took for his family ended up being taken away from some other prisoner, who perhaps went without.

As I drove her husband, General Saad, from Hoover 7 towards his wife in the waiting tent, I stopped the vehicle on the dirt road to have a couple of words with him. I told him, with kindness, that I hoped he understood what I was doing was outside of my normal duties and way outside of our camp rules. I didn't want him to expect this every week and I wanted to make sure he appreciated this gesture of kindness. I observed the rules and regulations of the MP unit managing the camp. Most of what I did for the generals was a long way from being within my normal duties, but was definitely not against the rules.

That night as I visited my generals, General Saad took me aside to offer up his prayer beads and several large rings as a token of appreciation for the many things I had done for him. He said he felt bad about the money I had given his wife the week before so she could return home from visiting him and for the many other acts of kindness performed. I wanted no gifts for my deeds, just a change of heart from him, to start thinking of others first, leaving his self-serving ways behind.

Imprisonment brings out the very worst and the very best in people. There were those who never asked for anything, always putting others before self. They were the same ones who never complained, never whined, and never cried about being there so long. They were the ones who made productive use of their time, finding ways to be productive in any situation. Those quiet but influential doers had an enormous impact on the lives of all those at Camp Bucca.

From time to time, I got up early to enjoy a sunrise. I was surprised that in that barren and desolate land they were beautiful beyond description. The oranges, yellows, and reds of dawn brought a burst of glorious color to an otherwise colorless setting. As the sun edged above the horizon, its radiance would dance across the desert floor bringing the hope of a new day. I realized that each morning brought us closer to our goal: the freeing and stabilizing of Iraq.

One evening, the generals were swarming around Major Price as he passed out a few special items he had been able to acquire. I took this opportunity to walk around the camp with General Hakim. We walked side by side, back and forth, across the front of the pen, far out of hearing distance of other prisoners. I was always so moved by his comments and his generosity. While the others were grabbing up stuff from Major Price, General Hakim declined to get anything for himself, saying that he would be last if there was anything left.

Hakim and the small group of men in his tent never asked for anything and were so humble about receiving things from us.

As we began our discussion, I felt a spiritual bond with him and commented on the way I was feeling. He concurred, stating he was feeling something different, too. We shared a unique bond of friendship, full of mutual trust, respect, and admiration. He had been blessed with a great attitude—optimism, compassion, and humility—uncommon in most men, especially army generals.

He was elated by the news that Coalition forces were building on many of the ideas he had developed and presented to me. He was ecstatic, not because they had followed his advice, but because he truly felt they were headed down the right course. He was full of hope for the success of the Coalition's endeavors.

General Hakim's next comments stunned me. He said he felt as if he were the student and I were the teacher. He felt he could learn so much from me and that together we could accomplish great things for the people of Iraq. I paused for a moment while casting my eyes down to my feet and feeling quite undeserving of his confidence in me. He reminded me of his pledge to be my shield from any would-be assailants if I were to go into Baghdad.

As I considered the task ahead, I felt truly inadequate in teaching him anything. I was the student who was learning from him. General Hakim was a pillar of stone, unmoved by the forces of men who tried to shake his conviction. My emotions crept close to the surface as I recognized that a caring God was guiding our efforts and our lives.

General Mahmood—Dark Eyes—was finally ready to be yanked around like a puppet on a string. He was so hammered from the prisoner-of-war experience that he was ready to do just about anything. We had him eating out of our hand. It had been a long road, but he had come around and was finally ready to cooperate.

He actually had great value to us because of his government connections, having met with Saddam Hussein and his sons on numerous occasions. Gaining him as a partner, he could become our eyes and ears on the street at a very high level. But in his case, it seemed highly unlikely that he would be helpful given his untrustworthy nature. It is amazing what can be accomplished with the right amount of psychological pressure, the right strategy, and the right conditions. Never at any time did I use force, torture, or pain to accomplish my goal.

I had been reading a number of disturbing articles from Amnesty International and the Red Cross lambasting our soldiers for mishandling Iraqi prisoners. They were accusing the U.S. of mistreating POWs, including actions bordering on torture of Iraqi detainees. One such article from Amnesty International stated: "Detainees continue to report suffering extreme heat while housed in tents, insufficient water, inadequate washing facilities, open trenches for toilets, no change of clothes, even after two months' detention."

Amnesty staff heard complaints that included prolonged sleep deprivation and detainees being forced to stay in painful positions or wear hoods over their heads for long periods. It was and has been a normal interrogation procedure to hood the prisoners to prevent them from becoming too aware of their surroundings while transferring and moving the prisoner around. It is important to segregate the prisoners and to prevent them from talking with each other.

As an intelligence officer and senior interrogation chief in two different internment facilities in two wars, I was troubled about these allegations in the face of our efforts to provide the best possible treatment and conditions for these detainees, while still trying to get valuable information out of them that would save lives and prevent further acts of violence against other human beings. Yes, the prisoners lived in extremely hot conditions, where the temperature inside the tents was over 120°F. I lived in their country right along side them. American officers and enlisted men and women all lived in the same kind of tents under the same conditions without air conditioning.

Complaints about crowded conditions were equally absurd. Camp Bucca, designed to house 10,000 prisoners at one time was almost pleasant with numbers down to around 1,000. The conditions were difficult for everyone living there, both POWs and American soldiers.

After the war ended, there were thousands of criminals who had been released from prison by Saddam. Within 90 days of the start of the war most of the military personnel held in Camp Bucca had been released, except for the generals and colonels in Hoover 7. This left in the camp only the worst type of criminals, who had been murdering,

Prisoners' solar shower at Camp Bucca.

stealing, raping, and committing various other crimes against the people of Iraq. What did they want the U.S. to do with these criminals? Put them back on the streets of Iraq?

Regardless of their status, rank, or crimes, we fed the prisoners plenty of food twice a day, food prepared right next to where my food was prepared. We made every effort to provide them with food of their own liking, ethnic food as close to their own as possible, prepared by people from that region of the world, purchased right from the local economy in that region.

We gave them new T-shirts, new jump suits, additional clothing whenever needed, slippers, flip-flops, socks, and much more. They received plenty of supplies. They had soap, shampoo, towels, and many other personal necessities. They were provided with cots to sleep on, blankets when necessary, and cot mattresses if wanted. The medics came by every morning to see if they had any ailments to report. They had daily showers, plenty of water, soccer balls, and many other items for their comfort, enjoyment, and benefit.

Camp Bucca was a prisoner of war camp, now transitioning to being a prison. If you were to look at a list of why the men were being detained, you would see that most of them were there because they had either committed some violent crime or had attempted to attack or kill an American. Regardless of their crimes, we continued to believe in their human rights and made every effort to consider their needs.

I have seen interrogation teams from all over the world conducting interrogations, witnessed firsthand their approaches and techniques, which has only reconfirmed my belief that the United States of America is one of only a few countries that honors the Geneva Convention. Without a doubt, we treat our prisoners better than anyone else in the world. Even the Iraqi generals commented in surprise and admiration on the treatment they received from us. They certainly wouldn't have been treated like this by Saddam Hussein.

In our interrogations, I never witnessed any physical abuse of the prisoners. We never used torture as means to acquire information, unless you consider taking away a prisoner's cigarettes cruel and unusual. I did make a prisoner sit out in the sun once for an hour. All of our techniques involve psychological methods of extracting information, viewing torture as an inefficient method to break people. No doubt, information can be extracted through torture, but its truthfulness would be questionable. Gaining the prisoners' trust and respect is by far the most effective method for gathering intelligence.

Our objective was to get life-saving information out of these people in an expeditious manner. This did require us to use a variety of well-established approaches and strategies. We made every effort to silence and segregate the prisoners when necessary to insure there was no collusion between prisoners. This might require us to hood them on occasion. We did strip search the prisoners to insure they were not carrying any weapons. We had to keep them on edge, unsure of their fate and fearful of their treatment.

There were exceptions and isolated incidents, but those were few and far between. If there was any mistreatment, it was rare and not representative of the thousands of prisoners who had received the best possible treatment.

We lived in a strange place, far away from what we knew and were familiar with. We were under a lot of stress from the conditions and demands placed upon us in that environment. We were dealing with a very strange element. We were surrounded by far-from-the-norm fundamentalists, fanatics, extremists, and hardened criminals. We were away from our loved ones back home, working long hours, with no days off. And more than anything, we were concerned about saving American lives.

I have seen nothing but the utmost respect for the prisoners' needs. In most cases we went out of our way to insure they were being handled appropriately. In many instances I personally witnessed genuine acts of kindness displayed towards the prisoners.

I held back from telling the generals until I knew for sure the date of my departure. I got the final definitive word on Monday and decided to inform the generals on Tuesday. I tried to push back my departure date for another week or so in order to finish up a few important things, such as writing a few more letters to key individuals petitioning the generals' release and taking care of Dark Eyes. I wanted to be at Camp Bucca when General Tarbet arrived from the States. But the word came down that I had to be in Baghdad by August 3 and there was no wiggle room.

Several of the generals had expressed a strong desire for me to stay with them until they were all released. They had pleaded with me to not allow anyone to move me until things had been resolved with their continued detention. I had tried to reassure them that no matter what, I would not forget them.

Tuesday night came too quickly. Major Price and I went together for me to say my final goodbyes to all the men in Hoover 7. When I arrived they were quick to come out of their tents, as if they had been notified of my pending departure. There was a certain uneasiness and uncertainty in the air. It was as if they knew what I was going to say.

I quickly made my way over to General Hakim who had not yet poked his head out of the tent. I wanted Hakim and the others in his tent to be the first to know of my schedule to leave.

I sat at the end of his cot while he and General Matta sat cross-legged on the ground, looking up as if to say, "Please, don't tell me you are leaving." Suddenly the words "I'm leaving," came tumbling out of my mouth. Then there was a long pause as I waited for their response. They both looked at me, then looked at each other, and simultaneously said, "This is not good news." They expressed their concern for my safety since I was going to Baghdad. They both promised to be there with me immediately following their release, to be my shield, and to pray for me continuously.

Looking through the tent door, noticing the others were gathering outside, I rose to my feet to say goodbye. With tears welling in my eyes, I embraced each of them and thanked them for the great example they had been to me and for the many things I had learned from them. They too were crying as I departed their tent, promising to see me again in Baghdad as soon as possible. I knew at that moment that we would be friends for life, with a bond that could not be broken. I love those men and regard them as my brothers.

I walked over to the rest of the group who were patiently sitting in a circle on a large piece of tent canvas. One single spot was reserved for me to sit next to General Shamil who had usually been my spokesperson. Major Price had already prepped the group by stating that I had something to tell them. General Shamil looked at me, ready to interpret my words; he knew what I was going through. He told the men that I would speak when I could, but they all knew why the words didn't come. When our eyes met, we all knew how final this goodbye would be.

I had grown close to so many of them. I had spent almost every night for three months getting to know them, seeing them at their worst and at their best, meeting their families, knowing their special needs, and working through bureaucratic frustrations. We were now brothers, held together with a bond uncommon in the course of most human lives.

The words came slowly as I attempted to express my feelings about them. As I looked around the circle, I recalled unique things about each man, hoping to burn their image in my memory. I felt confident that we would meet again under different circumstances. I knew many of them were destined to be the future leaders of Iraq.

I promised to continue the fight for their release, which was even more likely given the nature of my new assignment. I was moving to Baghdad to work at the top of the food chain, with all the bigwigs who were running the country. What better place for me to work for the generals' release. It was an answer to prayer. It couldn't have happened at a better time, since I had exhausted all available avenues to get them released. I was sure that at some point many of these men would be working with me in Baghdad.

Chapter Seven

Life in the Palace

Like many, I grew up equating Babylon with evil, excess, and idolatry. After my reassignment, I realized that I was being sent into the heart of evil. Geographically, biblical Babylon is about 50 miles south of Baghdad; morally, they are next-door neighbors. Everything bad I had ever connected to Babylon was twice as bad, or worse, under Saddam Hussein. It was strange to realize that this land of corruption had once been the first civilization to establish a written code of law under Hammurabi. Perhaps that meant that the rule of law could be re-established.

If I had tried to concoct the most dramatic change of assignment possible in Iraq, Bucca to Baghdad would have been it. Camp Bucca was about as far from the center of Iraq as possible, in the south near the Kuwaiti border and Iraq's sliver of a coastline. The area near Camp Bucca had been shunned by Saddam and his oil largess. The radio tower next to my sand-infested office and rooftop dormitory was about the most opulent architectural masterpiece Saddam ever bestowed on that desolate part of Iraq.

But now I was in Baghdad, smack-dab in the middle of Iraq. I was in the heart of Iraq, in the center of Baghdad and at the administrative epicenter of the new Iraq. Of Saddam's many presidential palaces, I was stationed in the main governmental palace, in what was once the nucleus of his regime. After the fall of Saddam it was called

Coalition Provisional Authority (CPA) Headquarters, formerly a palace of Saddam Hussein.

the Coalition Provisional Authority (CPA) Headquarters and was center stage for the Coalition's military and governmental operations. It was a massive complex of colossal, oversized buildings, all erected according to Saddam's presidential style. But all the marble, high ceilings, chandeliers, and handcrafted decorations in the world could never compensate for his lack of good taste. The difference between opulence and bad taste is that opulence has its limits. In Saddam's Iraq, bad taste hit new lows.

The CPA Headquarters was at the center of the Green Zone. Everything within a one-mile radius emanating from the CPA was considered a safe area. The area, consisting of governmental buildings and housing was cleared of would-be attackers and was secured, monitored, and patrolled by U.S. troops 24 hours a day.

My new position pushed me in a different direction. I was a strategic debriefer at the CPA. With the war's major combat operations completed, we were no longer capturing prisoners of war. Most of the POWs had been released, thus bringing about the change in my mission. As a debriefer, I interviewed people that had information they wanted to voluntarily share with the Coalition. These were average Iraqi citizens who had seen something, heard something, or knew something of importance relating to criminal activities, weapons, potential attacks, corruption, or any other activity against Coalition forces or the Iraqi people.

A good debriefer has a skill set similar to those of an interrogator, except the debriefer doesn't need to break the subject, or force them to talk by using certain approaches. The debriefer instead needs to determine the credibility of the source and the shared information.

Many good Iraqis were stepping forward to bring us information about activities going on against Coalition forces. Every day people came to our office to inform us of activities in their community that were illegal, that were pro-Saddam, or were in opposition to Coalition forces. We gathered the information from the sources and, as directed by General Sanchez, pushed the information to action. The required action would typically involve dispatching a team of Special Forces to conduct a raid on the location reported by the sources. These raids were conducted nightly often resulting in more information and more leads.

More gratifying than the opulence of my new surroundings was being able to work side by side with my long-time friend Chief Allen. America's first battle with Saddam brought us together in 1991 in Saudi Arabia during Desert Storm. We were similar in temperament, personality, and motivation. We had a synergy and compatibility that made working together an adventure in discovery and personal fulfillment.

Chief Allen and I were fortunate enough to snag a large second floor office for our two linguists and us. The office was about 40 feet long and 20 feet wide and was lit by two crystal chandeliers hanging from 15-foot ceilings. There were three large windows from which we could see one of the four large sculptured heads of Saddam that guarded the four corners of the building. But the centerpiece of our office was the Mother of All Desks. I'm sure it was originally slated for a much larger and more important office, perhaps for Ambassador Bremer. But for now it was all ours. Fortunately, we were able to procure six large high-backed chairs, perfect for dealing with the number of sources we had to talk to on a daily basis.

In spite of the palatial setting, I was actually humbled by the broad scope of the mission and the endless possibilities of this assignment. This new assignment provided a degree of flexibility that allowed me to call upon my own ingenuity and creativity to come up with solutions. I could develop new ways of gathering human intelligence from a variety of sources. The whole city of Baghdad was my playground. I was ready for this new challenge and hoped I was up to the task.

Home was a small but comfortable trailer located on the palace compound. As I sat on a real bed, listening to my boom box, I could reach over to my mini-fridge and grab a bottle of ice-cold water, all in a room cooled to a perfect temperature by my own AC unit. I almost felt guilty—almost.

The comforts of the palace shielded us from many of the natural elements of the desert, but when we went outside there was still the oppressive heat to contend with. Anytime we ventured beyond the walls of our compound we were required to wear full battle rattle, which was never comfortable but always comforting.

On my first full day at the palace, I went out with one of our collection teams to familiarize myself with the neighborhoods of Baghdad and scope out the area. We drove all over this sprawling city of five million.

I was able to witness firsthand the nature and the extent of the damage inflicted by the weaponry of the U.S. military. It was quite a tribute to the precision of our bombing to drive through a neighborhood and see only the targeted buildings completely demolished while adjacent buildings remained unscathed. Never, during our day of driving around Baghdad, did I see any evidence that our bombs had missed their targets, inadvertently hitting a house or a school or other civilian areas.

My interpreter continually remarked about how the city of Baghdad had changed since he was there many years ago. "The city used to be beautiful and clean, modern for its time, some 20 to 30 years ago," he said. "The city is now showing its age from the years of neglect and the scars of war. It's dirtier and more run down."

There was very little color to the buildings, the sandy khaki color dominated the landscape. There was a lot of trash and garbage on the sidewalks and streets, showing that not all services were operating.

Most of the city appeared to be up and running with electrical power restored. Although some of the shops and businesses were not yet open, many were, indicating that people were attempting to recover from a season of disruption caused by war. I was pleasantly surprised to see the people bustling around busily engaged in shopping, work, and other daily activities. The streets were full of cars and people, even congested at times, which was somewhat frightening in a land where traffic laws are widely disregarded.

We were always aware that at any moment an unseen assailant from a window or rooftop could light us up. We never forgot, even for a second, the ever-present danger of the areas we were traveling in—our loaded rifles were ready to fire. We were careful not to get blocked in by any of the traffic, using our Hummer's ability to drive over obstacles or to change direction immediately when the traffic started to jam up. After driving these streets daily for a few weeks, we started feeling comfortable about driving around in the middle of the day. I trusted the team chief's instinct regarding the degree of danger we were facing at any given moment.

At one safe area, we stopped to grab a few cold drinks from a friendly street vendor, who along with other Iraqi citizens thanked us for our willingness to come to their rescue. A man parked his car for a moment to buy some meat hanging in a butcher shop, so with my interpreter, I walked over to share some small talk with a young boy who had been left in the car. The boy, Talib, said he was six years old. In his cute smile and expressive eyes I could see a bright future.

The owner of the butcher shop came out to speak with us and spoke English quite well. He was curious about our presence in his neighborhood, but more than anything wanted to show off his ability to speak English. He said he used to teach at the university. He was quick to inform me that he was a Christian and no longer afraid to admit that.

Throughout our Baghdad excursion, we were greeted by the friendly waves and smiles of people on the street. Supposing they might be afraid of an imposing military vehicle and our weapons, I made a special effort to wave to everyone I could see as we drove around; I was making an effort to win over the Iraqi people any way I could.

A few days later, I had the opportunity to board a Black Hawk helicopter taking us to a meeting north of Baghdad. From my perch in the sky, I was able to get a full view of what Iraq was really all about. As I left the city, I saw an expanse of farms, fields, date palm groves, and countryside stretching toward the horizon. I saw herds of goats, cows, and sheep grazing in sparse fields of hay.

As we continued our flight further north, the cultivated green landscape gave way to more barren grazing land. There were adobe houses grouped together in flat-roofed villages, all sharing the same khaki color. The farm houses appeared poor, at times without power or running water. I saw canals bringing water from the two major rivers nearby, the Tigris and the Euphrates. Children would run out of their houses to wave as we passed overhead.

Before the invasion of Kuwait and the ensuing Gulf War, Iraq was supplying 80 percent of the world's trade in dates. Since 1991 the number of date trees in Iraq declined from 14 million to 4 million. Other agricultural exports also withered as Saddam used his oil revenues to fund a military buildup and wars with Iran and Kuwait. Now, Iraq's agricultural resources are only capable of meeting domestic needs.

Every night the sound of gunshots echoed throughout the city, reminding me of the ever-present danger that lurked around every corner. This random unpredictability kept us on our toes, wondering with every explosion if perhaps one of our fellow soldiers had just fallen.

Some days were worse than others as far as the number of attacks. Sometimes it was soldiers just being out at the wrong time in the wrong areas or behaving carelessly. Other times it was a car bomb or a remote-controlled detonation on a bridge or street.

The insurgent weapon of choice had become the Improvised Explosive Device (IED). An IED is a homemade device that can be detonated to kill, maim or harass anyone unfortunate enough to be nearby. An IED can be contained in almost anything—a milk carton, a can of soda, a dog carcass, a car, or a trash bag. An IED can be placed on the roadside, stashed in a pothole, taped to a car, stuffed in a building, set on a bridge or strapped to a person. Occasionally, they are simply tossed from a moving vehicle.

An IED can be time-delay triggered, command detonated by wire, or remotely detonated by a cell-phone, pager, doorbell button, key-fob, or toy-car remote. An IED can use homemade, commercial, or military explosives alone or in combination with toxic chemicals, biological toxins, or radiological material. Every IED is viciously unique in its design, manufacture, application, and potential for mayhem.

In 2004 there were almost 12,000 known IED-related incidents. For a small-time insurgent, an IED was less expensive than an AK-47, easier to put into action, and able to deliver more bang for the buck. Sometimes they were used simply to harass and discredit the security forces in Baghdad. Frequently they were used to entice Coalition forces into prepared ambushes. They were often used to target individuals or groups, also claiming the lives of countless civilians who happened to be standing in the way.

While I was there, IEDs became the single greatest threat Coalition forces faced in Iraq. Increasingly, they were also used against Iraqis who were cooperating with the Coalition, causing distrust and instability and fear. This underscored the value of gathering intelligence regarding these insidious and destructive devices. Whenever one was located and disarmed, we knew lives had been saved.

Thankfully, there were many safe areas around the city and the attacks were isolated. Most neighborhoods were peaceful and virtually without incident.

We received leads on who these terrorists were and in many cases we were able to take them down. On one of my first nights in Baghdad, we were able to catch up with a Fedayeen officer who had been terrorizing a neighborhood. It was a time-consuming process involving considerable assistance from the locals who were gaining confidence in our ability to provide security for Iraq. As the days went by, the locals trusted us more and more, which was evident by the number of people stepping forward to provide us with information.

We had numerous individuals stepping forward to divulge information but many times their real intent was to request a job, a favor or reimbursement for their time and expenses. I started to feel like everyone was looking to take care of themselves under the pretense of serving their country.

We had to assume ulterior motives unless our experience proved otherwise. I wasn't able to fully trust the information that was being shared by these sources until we had made some determination of their integrity and desire to serve their country. I recognized that many of these individuals were just trying to survive in a very difficult environment. Some of the Iraqi people were so desperate that for a handful of cash they were willing to fire on a soldier, blow up a tank, or set an explosive on a bridge. The various anti-Coalition groups were basically hiring poor peasants to pull the trigger to kill our soldiers. Many of those people served whatever side would pay them the most.

Day after day, we continued to meet with people who wanted to share information they had regarding things going on in the city. I was amazed by the number of absurdly bogus reports we received from people attempting to milk the system or get something for nothing. At times I wondered if I had the word "sucker" written in Arabic on my forehead. At times the information was just not as valuable as the person thought or didn't result in the compensation they were expecting.

One gentleman who assisted us was disappointed with the job offer we gave him, believing he was owed something more to his liking. I was disappointed with his attitude after I felt we had done all we could do. He gave no indication that he appreciated anything we were offering him, not even in a polite way of acknowledging our efforts. At times, I wondered if I would be able to remain compassionate as I continued to deal with my fair share of liars, ingrates, weaklings, bums, and sycophants.

Other times, it seemed like I was in some kind of a parent-child relationship, trying to get the Iraqis to step up to the plate, to be responsible, to take advantage of opportunities, and to take some initiative. But we knew where these people had been and what kind of environment they had grown up in for the last two and a half decades. Each day we saw the human harvest of Saddam's repressive regime.

The minds of these people had been brainwashed for so long that there was a huge gap between us and them. One of our interpreters told us of a time, several years earlier, when he was walking along the side of the road and people threw things at him as they drove by because he held a guitar in his hand. They told him that he would go to hell for listening to Western music and playing a Western instrument. Americans have a long way to go before we begin to understand the mind set of many Iraqis.

It was not that we wanted to force Western culture upon them, rather that we wanted to assist them in creating an environment of freedom and responsibility where they could initiate positive changes without fear of reprisal. We wanted to help them improve their standard of living and open the doors to freedom, enabling them to take their rightful place in the free world.

Scattered among all of the self-serving people with their ulterior motives were many sincere, hard-working Iraqis who just wanted to get on with their lives and see their country prosper. I spoke with a restaurant owner who had come in to give us some information. I asked him about his business, given the current situation. He replied that business was really tough, especially without electricity, but any kind of business was better than life with Saddam. He invited us over to dine whenever we got a chance.

I also recall a mother and her daughter who had both found work in the new government. They were grateful for our efforts and invited us to spend some time at their farm on the outskirts of Baghdad, to enjoy some real home cooking and a ride on their boat on the Tigris River.

Two Iraqi policemen were kind enough to bring in some baked chicken, hummus, flatbread, olives, and pickled cucumbers. I relished every bite of it, appreciating their delicious offering, which was a pleasant change from our normal lunch of corn dogs or tuna fish sandwiches. They brought us enough to share with anyone else that had the good fortune of dropping in on our office picnic. We spread it out on the table normally used for maps and other more important matters.

Iraqis like these recognized that Americans brought hope to this land and its people. Freedom and hope are contagious and I made it my aim to spread that light to every Iraqi I came in contact with. Americans are an optimistic people and we are eager to share freedom with the world. As one British interrogator said to me, "You Americans really do have hope for this land, don't you?" You bet your life we do.

It was almost 8:30 PM and I was up in my big office wrapping up my day's work. As I looked out from my windows, I could see that darkness had fallen on another day in Baghdad. The sun had just crept beyond the horizon, leaving a slight glimmer of light behind the skyline.

The sounds of gunshot could be heard sporadically around the city, as the cover of darkness provided refuge for would-be attackers. Most of the city was quiet, tired from a long day of struggling to make ends meet. Parts of the city were forced to retire early due to the lack of electricity. It was frustrating to lay down electrical wiring only to have it stolen or damaged the next day by thieves and other thugs.

In the mornings, I ran to the perimeter of the compound and around the building to put in my two or three miles. It was a quiet running course interrupted only by the familiar sounds of Army vehicles driving by. That morning a couple of tanks turned in front of me as they commandeered a corner.

Most of the buildings in the palace compound were empty, except for a few Army units who had claimed part of it as their territory. Several of the buildings were uninhabitable, bombed into a pile of concrete rubble and twisted steel. In the undamaged buildings, I was amazed that there was still much to admire in the intricate designs and the craftsmanship of the marble and wood, in spite of its gaudy tastelessness. As I started to become familiar with some Arabic letters, I began to notice Saddam Hussein's initials woven into almost every pattern, design or decorative motif.

The streets were wide and lined with palm trees; massive concrete arches served as gates into the area. In its glory days this palace was a real showplace for Saddam.

Early in the mornings when I was out running in the deserted streets of the Green Zone or late in the day when I was finally able to retreat to the comfort of my trailer, I noticed a welcome change in the outside temperature. There finally seemed to be signs of relief from the relentless summer heat. I'm not saying it was cool, only that the highs had started to come down ever so slightly. There was a feeling in the air that a shift in the weather pattern was on its way.

There were many in Iraq who feared change and distrusted it. They resisted the changes that had to take place with Saddam gone. They looked at change with apprehension and reluctance. It goes without saying that change can be painful, sorrowful at times, and difficult. Change is the very thing we were hoping to initiate in this tightly closed part of the world.

Days later, as I was going about my work, I heard and felt a large blast not far away. Loud blasts were a fairly common occurrence, so I wasn't too alarmed until later when I returned to the office to hear that the UN headquarters had been destroyed by a truck bomb, killing 24 people including top envoy, Sergio Vieira de Mello.

There was an unusual buzz around the CPA as people grabbed bits of information related to the bombing. I was saddened to learn that so many people had been killed or injured. This added to my concern for all of our soldiers in harm's way. It was even more unsettling to discover that many innocent bystanders, people looking for work, and a variety of others had fallen victim to this latest act of senseless brutality.

Many of the acts of terrorism were being committed by non-Iraqis who had traveled there for the sole purpose of disrupting our efforts to give those people a life free from fear, bondage, and torture. These acts of violence only strengthened our resolve to continue in our efforts to help create a land of security and freedom.

Much of the Coalition's accomplishments was going largely unnoticed by the media. Schools and hospitals had been opened, playgrounds and housing projects had been started, and many jobs had been created. Where was all the talk about the thousands of good things that had been done? Why were the media not getting out the word that many great and positive things were occurring every day? This remained a constant source of irritation.

Chief Scott "Authentico" Allen in the palace.

Chief Allen and I played tag-team humor with our interpreters and sources on occasion, adding a little levity to our experience there. Being able to joke around and make fun of things helped us get through this extended time away from our families. Humor was a great anesthetic, numbing us from the stark reality of where we were and what we were doing. It was comforting that we could feed off each other for humorous sustenance, satisfying our need to make light of a difficult situation.

We just didn't want to take things too seriously, realizing that life for so many in Iraq was too painful to discuss, many of them just barely able to go on day after day. The truth of their bleak existence would have been depressing to many. I was astonished that they could go on for so long without any income; many of them had yet to return to any kind of paying work.

There is a commonly used phrase that captures the attitude of many of the people in Iraq and much of the Islamic world: *Inshallah* meaning "God willing" or "if God wills it." Almost every comment regarding a future occurrence is followed by the phrase "*Inshallah.*" Even something as simple as, "I'll see you tomorrow" is couched with the "God willing" caveat. This often seems to replace hope with a fatalistic recognition that the future is out of their control.

In the course of my interviews with numerous sources, I was surprised by how many of them, in their 30s and 40s, felt their life was on the downhill slide or basically over. It was astonishing to me how a young man in his early 30s could think for a moment that his life was the way it was going to be without much hope for anything different or better.

Conversely, if someone were to ask me what was sustaining those people who were able to rise above such a harsh environment, I would have to say it was hope—hope of a new beginning, hope for a brighter future, hope for a free Iraq.

One of our young Iraqi interpreters, Hussain, conveyed to me an incident he recently had with his family who asked about the Americans he was working with. He said, "The one thing that stands out about Americans is that they have a lot of hope for things to come." He went on to say, "They believe in the power of hope and are attempting to give hope to us." Initially, it was in short supply, but I saw it growing.

In coming to my new position at the CPA, I was blessed to be working for the U.S. Army general responsible for approving the discharge of the Iraqi generals still held at Camp Bucca. I continued to actively push forward the meticulous paperwork necessary to secure their release. This required working through the many layers of military bureaucracy, completing each step with accuracy. After all the paperwork was submitted, 12 of my 14 generals were approved for immediate release. This was wonderful for them, wonderful for their families, wonderful for me, and wonderful for the future of Iraq.

My position at the palace also gave me the opportunity to work with Lieutenant Colonel Sarna who was responsible for rebuilding the Iraqi military. I told him about the generals at Camp Bucca and what a great asset they would be in helping us to achieve our rebuilding goals. I expounded on all their experience, background, their willingness to help, and the amount of trust I had for each one of them. I was doing a real sales job on him, almost wishing I had each of their résumés to give him.

Feeling the spirit of my words, Colonel Sarna agreed to talk with me further about the generals. He put me in contact with an Australian officer in charge of rebuilding the Iraqi Air Force, who soon dropped by my office to chat about the value of using my prisoner generals as consultants.

The Australian officer was especially interested to hear about my dear friend General Hakim. I was enthusiastic as I elaborated on his experience and the general's desires to be involved in rebuilding the Iraqi military. Before I left Camp Bucca, I took the time to ask the generals what they would like to do the most when they were released. General Hakim told me his greatest desire was to help rebuild the Iraqi Air Force.

As I sat across the desk with the man responsible for creating the new Iraqi Air Force, I could hardly contain my exuberance and I could see he was getting the message. After lunch he left for awhile only to return with the approval to move quickly to get General Hakim released and up to Baghdad to help get the process moving. I was amazed by what I was hearing; it couldn't have been more perfect.

The monumental Saddam busts which once graced the four corners of the CPA palace had been dislodged and were placed face down in the dirt awaiting transport to another location. There was a sign written in both Arabic and English, posted by the heads which advised, "Do not urinate on." It was tempting, but we obeyed the sign.

Every day as I interviewed source after source, I was reminded of what life there was really like outside the marble and ornately carved walls of the palace, beyond the plush green trees and high steel barricades. All day long I entertained sources bringing forth the worst possible news of the trouble running in the streets of that country. I heard story after story of weapons dealers in their neighborhoods, counterfeiting operations around the corner, stockpiles of weapons in people's bedrooms, anti-Coalition meetings going on, people trying to build up armies against us, attacks on our soldiers, criminal acts going on just down the street, illegal smuggling from neighboring countries, extortion rings, people wanting permits to arm themselves, stolen property being sold, and aircraft being hidden. That was what I listened to all day long.

One guy came in under the guise of having a friend who heard on the radio that Coalition forces were giving rewards for weapons being turned in. He was actually an arms dealer trying to find out if he could sell the weapons to me. He had also studdied black magic and parapsychology and fancied himself as somewhat of an expert on telling the future. Imagine his discouragement when I told him we were not in the arms business and not willing to work with arms dealers. He went on and on about how we were making so many mistakes in dealing with the problems at hand. He ranted that the U.S. was not doing this right and not doing that right, saying we weren't taking care of all Iraqi problems.

I had heard enough. So I let him have it, gently, of course, asking him, "Why aren't you doing something to eradicate some of the ills polluting your society instead of selling arms to people trying to kill us? Why aren't you and your friends doing your part? As patriotic Iraqi citizens, your should be working to rid the country of some of its problems."

I told him we weren't in Iraq to be out front leading the way while Iraqis sit in their homes waiting for new jobs and money to drop in their laps. We expected to see the Iraqi people rise to the occasion. I looked him straight in the eye and said, "This is your country and it is your responsibility to deal with the problems at hand. It's time to get to work."

He actually took it well, acknowledging his role in contributing to the problem and confessing he should be doing something positive instead of dealing in the black market. I felt encouraged by his response—until he asked me if I could help him get his former job back, hoping I would write a letter of recommendation to his ex-boss. I should have known he had something else up his sleeve.

A few days later, this arms-dealing parapsychologist had been reborn—well, sort of. All of a sudden he declared his interest in doing what he could legally do to help, doing what was right to bring about some solutions to the problems facing his country. He was singing a different tune, actually attempting to act as somewhat of a partner with us. He suggested bringing in his relative, an ex-Iraqi intelligent officer, to meet with us.

Soon all of us were seated around the Mother of All Desks in our palace office: the born-again parapsychologist weapons dealer, the ex-Iraqi intelligence officer, three interpreters, Chief Allen, and I. It was a strange gathering with an unknown agenda. I wondered if anything valuable could possibly emerge.

We spent the next two hours listening to all the great things the intelligence officer had done for the regime and how badly Saddam had treated him in return. Basically, we had a disgruntled regime employee now hoping to deliver some payback to his old buddies from the intelligence agency. It was painful at times just trying to stay awake as we gave up trying to direct the discussion with our questioning. It was venting time for this heavy-set secret agent, who continued to eat all the treats we had laid out and chain-smoked one cigarette after another.

During the meeting, the parapsychologist was sending me cues and signals, one time even motioning for me to step outside to discuss how he thought I should proceed with his uncle's questioning. After we finally got the two of them to wrap up their whining, I grabbed my Kevlar helmet and flak jacket to drive them back to the front gate of the Green Zone where they were parked. I wasn't interested in meeting with them again any time soon.

On another occasion, I received a call from the front gate regarding some people who showed up to talk to me. Grabbing my gear and interpreter, we went out to pick them up. There were two Iraqis, one a former intelligence officer and the other a former brigadier general. The intelligence officer started out by saying he had several Saddam tapes he had looted from a government building during the fall of Baghdad and now wanted to sell those to me. He had 100 tapes, thinking he could solicit $50 a piece from me.

I quickly lost interest in both of them, prejudging that they were both there to make a quick buck, disappointed in their motives, and tired of the continual barrage of people wanting to help their country by selling me something. I wasn't interested in paying $5,000 for tapes which even he hadn't listened to. It was an ill-conceived attempt to get something for nothing. I nipped the tape sale in the bud, asking instead that he bring in a sample for me to listen to.

Now it was Brigadier General Abdullah's turn. I braced myself for the expected whining, griping, and finger-pointing. But on second glance, I could tell in Abdullah's face that this encounter would be different, pleasantly different. It seemed that whenever I would start to choke on the polluted air of selfish opportunists, someone would show up to give me a breath of fresh air. It was thrilling to find a trustworthy source, someone with moral fiber who cared about his homeland and wanted to help make it better—someone with no hidden agenda and no ulterior motives—a true patriot. These were the Iraqis who were willing take the steps necessary to become catalysts for a reformed Iraq. As his story unfolded, I saw true leadership.

Abdullah proceeded to tell us of his terrible ordeal with the old regime. Several years earlier he had spoken out against Saddam, attempting to gather support from other generals. Unfortunately, one of them turned him in to Saddam. Allegations of treason kept him under surveillance for some time, and he was ultimately placed in solitary confinement in the very palace we occupied. He spent three years of his life languishing in a small room in the basement of our building.

General Abdullah described in detail the extent of his ordeal, showing us while he spoke, the scars of the electrical torture he was subjected to. My interpreter and I sat in awe as we listened to the horrifying experience. At the end of three years, he was given a chance to recant all he had said and done against Saddam, but he wouldn't, and consequently was sent to Abu Ghraib Prison for another two years. He was stripped of his rank and retirement. Upon his release, he had no job and nowhere to go. His wife, humiliated by her husband's imprisonment, had taken the two children and moved away to another Arab country. He had lost everything.

With the fall of Saddam, Abdullah was finally able to step forward and openly tell his story. He was unshackled and free to fulfill his destiny in serving the people of Iraq. He had come to my office to offer up his assistance, unsure of how to proceed.

What a contrast in the two individuals sitting before me, one wanting to sell his loot to make a quick buck, the other humbly offering up his support for our efforts, anxious to assist us in any way possible. I was quick to point out the difference to both of them, hoping the tape salesman might have a change of heart, which he did.

I then turned to the general and commended him for his courage. Saddam had killed people for lesser crimes, including many that had spoken out against him. I was impressed that the general had not given up the fight, even when he had the chance to regain everything by just renouncing what he had said. He stayed the course and would not give in.

As I spoke to the general, I could see Renda, my interpreter, struggling to get out the words as she was moved to tears. We tried to communicate our appreciation for individuals like him who had the moral courage to do the right things for the right reason, not for personal gain or thoughts of compensation.

We saw a steady stream of people in our office who were well aware that the squeaky wheel gets the grease. They felt that if they were not complaining about the progress of things, then people would have a tendency to stop working on their issues. For the most part they were impatient with progress and emotional about their issues.

With their economy in shambles, people started to create an economy based on anything that could be sold. Even ordinary citizens were getting into the weapons business because there was supply and demand. Before the war began, Saddam made sure there were plenty of weapons available by unloading dump trucks full of weapons in neighborhoods. Iraq needed to develop other industries that would give people jobs and another source of income.

One day a young Iraqi man, whom we had met with on several previous occasions, came to our office. He was being threatened because of his job with the Americans. A local gang was threatening to kill him and his family if he did not resign from his position. The gang was also involved in extortion and selling weapons and drugs.

The young man came to our office to offer up any information that might help us in taking down a notorious and dangerous gang. We were attempting to hook him up with a Special Forces team in order to do a drive-by to identify the gang members' houses.

I knew the young man was engaged to be married in two weeks. I had seen his engagement party pictures, talked to him about his future wife, but felt something wasn't quite right. He didn't seem excited; quite the contrary, he appeared afraid and nervous.

As we delved into it further, feeling some fatherly instincts, I discovered he was not in love—in fact he didn't even like his fiancée. His mother arranged the marriage with the parents of the young lady, who was only 18 years old. Arranged marriages are still common in Iraqi society.

He had met his wife-to-be on several occasions and actually made every effort to discourage her from wanting to marry him. He admitted that on his visits, he went in his dirtiest clothes, smelling quite badly. He was rude to her, impatient, and obnoxious. He said he did everything he could to change her plans, but to no avail.

He described her as being somewhat spoiled, annoying, and quite a nag. He said he couldn't get her to shut up. She would constantly get on his case about a variety of things. As he put it, he was doomed, for he saw no way to get out of this predicament. He had even told her that as soon as he found someone he was truly in love with, he was going to marry a second wife, since Muslim men can have up to four wives. Even so, she was not budging nor changing her mind.

He explained that his mother had already found wives for his two older brothers, who were both unhappy with the choices she made for them. I felt badly for him, knowing his life was going to be difficult. I couldn't offer up any words of advice to help him, other than asking him to promise not to hit her, since physical abuse is a serious problem in many marriages in Iraq.

Our work with individuals on such a personal level often put us at the center of emotionally heated squabbles. One of my sources, who worked as a linguist at the palace, came in one day upset about gossip spreading through our work area. Someone had started a rumor that he was the pimp for a couple of sisters working in one of the ministries there. The scandalous tale was absolutely unfounded, absurd, and untrue. He was angry and determined to find out who was spreading such a vicious rumor, causing him shame and embarrassment.

He was a small man with enormous emotions. He was prepared to kill the culprit for their slander. It took me some time to calm him down to the point that reason and logic could prevail.

A few days later we got a call from the MPs at the front gate informing us that a young man around 30 years old was saying he was a former Fedayeen officer surrendering to Coalition forces. As expected, we jumped into action as soon as we heard the words "Fedayeen officer" and "surrender" used in the same sentence. We sent a team with handcuffs and a hood to detain the individual.

He was taken to our palace location for further questioning. Understandably, he was scared to death, breaking into tears on several occasions during the process. During his interrogation, we discovered that his mother had sent him to speak with us, hoping he could get a job and his back pay as a Fedayeen soldier. He had brought with him a résumé—typed in English no less—in hopes of gaining employment.

I felt so badly for this young fellow who came with high hopes, coaxed by his mother, thinking we were in the business of giving out jobs to ex-Fedayeen soldiers. You just don't want to come to the front gate of a compound saying "Fedayeen officer" and "surrender." I made sure he wasn't detained and gave him $20 for his trouble.

As usual, I was wakened early by the sound of the date palm branches outside my trailer scraping across the top of the trailer, dropping golden date nuggets on the roof. It sounded as if I were being pelted by shrapnel from a nearby explosion. As the bright rays of morning streamed through my trailer window I felt there was hope for a new beginning for Iraq. I went to my knees to offer up the gratitude of my heart for all that was transpiring around me as I personally witnessed the remaking of a nation, knowing we were not alone in our efforts. Humbly, I asked for help in being able to do my part in pushing this work forward. Of course, I knew the strange parade of characters that would soon be marching through my office.

One of the sources I was working with, Ali, brought his family from their home south of Baghdad, for the sole purpose of having dinner with Chief Allen, our interpreters, and me that evening. He and his family wanted to show their appreciation for all that we had been doing to help the Iraqi people.

We made our way across the 14th of July Bridge to meet them on the other side, outside of the Green Zone. They were waiting in front of the checkpoint there, ten people crammed into the cab of a small Nissan two-seater pickup, except for Ali's oldest son who was sitting in the back with the food.

We motioned for them to follow us as we gained approval from the guards for them to enter the Green Zone. We took them over to the Al-Rasheed Hotel, my late-night disco-dancing location, where we had received permission from the hotel management to have our dinner out by the pool. The Al-Rasheed was Saddam's hotel, being the closest one to his government buildings. It was a high-class hotel built by a Swiss company to provide plush accommodations for Saddam's visitors.

The pale blue pool was large, surrounded by an open area with plenty of white metal pool furniture for us to have our dinner on. It was completely unoccupied, but gave a sense of opulence in its grand size. A massive rectangle, it was three feet deep at one end and 15 feet deep at the other end where the diving platform was. A long bar served a variety of cocktails, sodas, and snacks, making it the perfect place for our gathering.

September meant the worst of the heat had passed and a slight breeze provided the perfect ambiance for a dinner together. Date-palm trees swayed in the evening air and many large shrubs, which hid us from any outsiders, surrounded the pool area.

Ali's family was beautiful; he and his wife, their children ranging in age from 9 to 16, his mother-in-law, his sister-in-law, and his brother-in-law's wife with her three-year-old daughter. What a wonderful Iraqi family—intelligent, well-mannered, neatly dressed, and full of optimism. All of them spoke enough English to introduce themselves and even understand some of what we were saying, although we had Russell, Renda, and Linda, three of our interpreters, just in case. We had a wonderful evening under the stars with delicious food and good friends.

About a week after our dinner I met with Ali and was saddened to discover there had been an attempt to kill him on his way to our office. There was a contract out on him due to his efforts to take down some of the anti-Coalition organizers in his area. It really disturbed me to learn of the risk he was incurring and the danger of his travels. I offered to give him more firepower if we could just get a weapons permit for him. This would put the odds more in his favor.

As we finished up our meeting, the sun was setting and I was quite concerned about Ali's welfare, especially after having met his family and his beautiful children. I warned him to be careful, even coaxing him to stay the night in Baghdad so as to not make the treacherous journey to his house at night. He declined and ventured out past the border of the Green Zone unprotected.

I was relieved a few days later to learn Ali had made it home safely that night and that subsequently his would-be killers had been arrested.

It was business as usual as I went to meet a new contact at the North Gate of the Green Zone. While examining the crowd that morning, I heard an unusual sound. At least it was unusual for that part of town.

There was a child crying somewhere behind the barbed wire that separated us from the throngs of people waiting for their chance to speak with someone. I scanned across the human ocean to see where the crying noise was coming from. The people that lined up each day normally had some civil matter that needed to be settled, so the crowd was almost exclusively male. Occasionally there would be a woman, but almost never a child. I was naturally curious, especially as the sound persisted.

Finally I located her—a young girl, maybe seven years old, separated from her mother and swallowed up by the crowd. But where was her mother? Visitors are granted permission to enter the secured area one at a time and only the first few had entered. I turned and saw a middle-aged Iraqi woman hobbling on crutches with only one leg. She had apparently left her young daughter outside to wait. The little girl was understandably frightened.

Once I spotted her trembling, scrawny frame, I quickly instructed the MPs to move the barbed wire back to let her join her mother. Her crying stopped as she darted to grab hold of her mother's long black dishdasha, torn and frayed from years of use. As she clung tightly to her mother's dress, I moved over slowly to brush her dark hair away from her eyes and to pat her gently on the head.

Her poverty was painfully evident as I surveyed her tattered dress and worn out plastic flip-flops. Her tangled black hair was matted against her head, indicating she had not had a bath in some time. Her skin was cracked and blistered from exposure to the scorching sun and constant wind. Tear tracks were visible on her dirty face.

As I crouched down to look into her eyes, a lump got caught in my throat. What could I possibly do to relieve this child's suffering? Then I remembered a box of goodies back in my office that might be just the ticket for this little girl.

I asked the guards to hold the girl and her mother there until I returned. Jumping into my SUV, I scrambled back to my office and rummaged through a FedEx box full of toys and trinkets sent by my teammates back home. I grabbed a comb, brush, toothbrush, toothpaste, flip-flops, whistle, and a stuffed monkey whose long arms and Velcro hands could hang around her neck. I dashed out the door, inviting my interpreter to come along.

As I made my way back to the gate, I saw the little girl and her mother waiting patiently. Bending down, I handed her each item with a smile and a brief explanation. As I gave her the toothbrush, I asked her to be sure to brush every day.

Her eyes lit up with delight as I put the monkey's arms over her head. Although somewhat shy, having not dealt with an American soldier before, I could see the excitement in her face as her big brown eyes looked up at me. I walked away quickly so as to not bring too much attention to the little girl. This spontaneous gesture had pretty much drained my "treasure chest."

What a moment! I had the chance to influence Iraqis one heart at a time. What might the ripple effect be from my effort to calm the tears of one Iraqi child? I returned to my office to express thanks to my teammates in the U.S. who had sent the original box of toys. What a truly inspired idea.

I had only one request of them—please send more toys.

Chapter Eight

Chief Wiggles

I was abruptly wakened from my restful sleep by the unmistakable crackle and rumble of explosions going off nearby, reminding me of exactly where I was. Awakening to the sound of rocket-propelled grenade explosions is not the best way to begin the day. I soon found out that the Al-Rasheed Hotel, just a few blocks away, had been hit by two rounds. The Al-Rasheed Hotel housed civilian Coalition officials and some U.S. military personnel. It was a symbol of security within the Green Zone. The attack caused minimal damage and no casualties, but it highlighted the vulnerability of even heavily guarded facilities within the Green Zone. I laid in bed for awhile, wondering how someone could have gotten so close to the hotel, deep in the heart of a secure area.

After being awakened by explosions, then hammered by a full day of frustrating and pretty unproductive interviews, I suspect my patience started to wear thin by late afternoon. My last appointment was at 6 PM with Ali, whose family and companionship we enjoyed so much the week before at the Al-Rasheed Hotel. Ali was accompanied by his boss, who along with his brother, were members of the Iraqi Governing Council.

I should have known by the way the meeting started that I was in for a ride. Ali's boss came out of the chutes with both guns blazing as he declared in an agitated voice that I had a trust issue with him. I told him it wasn't that I didn't trust him, but in that I had just met him, my trust would grow over time as we worked together. He found that modus operandi insulting.

I told him, "I trust you because of the trust I have for Ali. If he trusts you, I trust you." I let him know that at some point I would be able to have total trust for him independent of my friend, Ali. He wasn't pleased with my answer, expecting me to trust him unconditionally because of his family lineage and their 2,000-year-old tribal history.

In the three-hour rant that followed, he disparaged our efforts, saying that nothing was being done to fix Iraq's troubles and that the Coalition was not solving problems fast enough to satisfy him. Already weary from the day's activities, my patience began to wane and my personal defensive measures began to rear up as he raked the Coalition over the coals in a very direct and personal attack.

Here we were putting our lives on the line every day, away from our families for perhaps over a year, making great personal and financial sacrifices so that the people of his country could reap the benefits of freedom for the first time in their lives—and this guy had the nerve to say that we were not doing enough. My blood was now beginning to boil, but I made every effort to maintain my professionalism and calm demeanor.

He persisted with his rambling rebuke claiming that we were to blame for members of the Governing Council being targeted and even shot at. This was particularly absurd given the fact that the Governing Council represented the new government of Iraq, and as such were a threat to all those who were in the old regime.

He grumbled that his brother and he were considering resigning from the council because they lacked faith in the ability of the United States to resolve their problems and be successful in the endeavor. He felt it would be a blemish on their great family tribe if the U.S. failed.

I was caught off-guard by his tribe-over-nation mentality. He had neither the patience nor desire to contribute—much less sacrifice—in order to build a free Iraq. But he continued to stress that his personal honor was more important than the building of a free Iraq.

At this point, I was appalled and disgusted with his pompous, arrogant attitude. I imagine he was so willing to speak his mind because he had nothing to lose. Ali, who had remained quiet up till this point, made an attempt to come to my rescue as his boss persisted to pursue his attack on me. But his boss would not hear of it, telling Ali in Arabic to shut up and to not say another word. I felt sorry for Ali and could sense the pain and embarrassment from his boss's remarks.

I was losing it fast. I finally had to leave the room to regain my composure. I grabbed my partner, Chief Allen, who just happened to be passing by, and asked that he take my place until I could compose myself.

I returned after a few minutes, attempting to regain control of the conversation, finish up the meeting, and get this arrogant lout out of my office. As he was going to the door, he thrust in his final dagger when he said he was prohibiting Ali from seeing any of us again until his demands were met. That concerned me, knowing how valuable Ali's information had been.

As they were all leaving, Ali slipped me a note saying he would come to my office the next day to discuss what had happened.

When Ali returned the next day he was gushing with apologies. He stated repeatedly how his boss had no concept of what was happening and was clueless about the real situation. He wanted nothing to do with his boss and his boss's brother, convinced that they didn't have what was required to lead Iraq. Ali was leaving them for good, confident that he could find other people who were willing to work with him to make his dreams become a reality.

Knowing he was obtaining his livelihood from his boss, I told Ali I wanted to make a donation to his cause by giving him a couple hundred dollars, hoping that he would be willing to take the money under the pretense of his building community support for a free Iraq. At this point my interpreter, Renda, started to choke up as she attempted to interpret our sincere expressions of friendship for each other.

The following day Ali popped in for a second to drop off two bunches of plastic flowers his daughters had put together in an effort to cheer me up. I was touched by their kind gesture and knew that Ali had the moral courage to act independently of his boss.

At times I felt like I was holding a fishing pole with a whale at the other end, running out the line. I woke several times during the night with my mind bouncing around from one pressing issue to the next. I woke with my fishing line racing uncontrollably, fully engaged in the schedule of the day

In the midst of reeling in this whale, I found respite in being able to provide some assistance to individuals with urgent needs. One afternoon found me in our military hospital taking the young son of one of my sources to be evaluated by a neurosurgeon. The little boy was suffering from a seizure disorder, at least according to the Iraqi doctors. The child's condition had been worsening over the last few days, forcing us to take action and provide additional evaluation to get some type of care for his condition.

I met with the doctors a few days earlier to arrange for the appointment. The doctors were more than willing to help out due to the nature of the circumstances. I was pleased with their attitude, so gracious and eager to be of assistance. The doctor spent over two hours evaluating the little boy's condition, even to the extent of taking a CT scan. They were somewhat limited by the lack of certain equipment, but the doctor's prognosis was favorable, indicating that the condition didn't appear to be epilepsy.

While I was waiting for the doctor to complete his evaluation I walked outside to get some fresh air. Passing by the young American guard at the front of the hospital, I offered up the customary greeting, "How are you?" Her response caught my attention, compelling me to turn around and sit down next to her. After further inquiry, she broke down and started to cry, expressing how homesick she was.

In an effort to cheer her up I told her I'd return with a box of toys for her to pass out to the children that came to the hospital. Her eyes lit up and she smiled upon hearing my offer. Maybe that would take her mind off her own separation from loved ones.

At any given time I was pursuing numerous leads which, if proven to be true (and that was a huge *if*), would solve many of the various problems that existed in Iraq. Information poured in daily on the whereabouts of Saddam, the location of weapons of mass destruction, and stashes of gold. We would often get tips on the locations of Fedayeen, Wahhabi, Baath Party members, Mujuhadeen, ex-intelligence officers who were still pro-Saddam, and Al Qaeda members. Additionally, we would sometimes get information on potential attacks or bombs under bridges that, when acted upon, could save lives—Iraqi and American.

One night, a typical evening really, we met with Dr. Asani, who was campaigning to be the next president of Iraq, tribal sheikhs from five different family groups, two metaphysical spiritual leaders, a Kurdish lawyer, and an engineer/lieutenant colonel from the old regime. It was a kaleidoscope of diversity when you consider all of their idiosyncrasies, cultural traditions, religious beliefs, rituals, superstitions, and fears. Fortunately, they weren't all in the same room at the same time.

During one of my meetings with an especially helpful source, we both noted the many new opportunities that Iraqis would have with the removal of Saddam. We recognized that what the Iraqi people needed more than anything else was economic opportunity. With the lifting of the sanctions came increased opportunities for trade. Petroleum revenues could now be used to fund industrial and economic expansion rather than weapons, palaces, and an oversized military. The Iraqi people needed jobs, careers, incomes, benefits, and a vision for the future that included economic prosperity.

One of the sticky problems facing Iraq was that illegal activities constituted a substantial economic sector and seemed to be growing larger daily. Dealing in illegal weapons and munitions was bringing in great sums of money to finance operations and recruiting for anti-Coalition efforts. It was estimated that, on the oil pipeline alone, the country was losing millions of dollars a day through theft that directly funded anti-Coalition operations. The bad guys in Iraq were well organized and well funded. They offered their fellow citizens, people who were struggling to feed their families, a way to make ends meet by firing a shot or planting a bomb. Economic expansion and industrial growth could provide honest, responsible citizens a chance to opt out of the weapons business and plant their future in a sustainable business venture.

The U.S. military didn't have resources to pay the good guys to run operations against the bad guys, or provide resources for teams to go out and take down an insurgent group. We had a rewards program, but it was cumbersome and time consuming, not offering enough immediate compensation for good actions that would save lives.

Almost all of our sources were in need of something: a job, a reward, a phone, a mentor. Their willingness to work with us often represented a considerable sacrifice. They wanted to do good things for their country but were often unable to sustain themselves and continue their efforts without some form of compensation. They had to take care of their families first, making sure their children had food to eat and clothes to wear.

I found it especially productive to help our sources start up their own businesses, which would create jobs and income for them and other Iraqis. We had the ministries and other resources available to assist and teach them how to do it. We could even provide small business loans and other financial aid to help them start up new industries, which would help them escape from the temptation to get involved in illegal activities.

This approach helped us achieve multiple objectives. First, it helped provide needed jobs and income for Iraqis. Second, it provided an alternative to falling prey to the enticements of counterfeiters, gun runners, and drug dealers. Third, it fostered economic vitality within their community, giving hope and setting an example. Fourth, it began to strengthen the Iraqi economy, providing goods and services that could be exported to other countries. Long term, this would help Iraq to regain a foothold in the international economic community.

I had already implemented this approach with two of my sources that had the capabilities, the skills, and the knowledge to be successful. There were abundant opportunities for Iraqi entrepreneurs to bid as subcontractors on projects such as remodeling buildings, cleaning up rubble, disposing of scrap metal, demolition, and other valuable and productive projects. I was invigorated by the vision of what capitalism and hard work could do for their country. Most of the Iraqi entrepreneurs and small businessmen I met were energetic and full of ideas to make their business ventures successful. The possibilities were endless and the benefits were immense.

★

Throughout my time in Iraq, I had been keeping a journal of my experiences. Initially, I emailed these journal entries to friends and family. Eventually, a friend suggested that it would be easier to post the notes on the internet for everyone to see at once. He helped me set up an internet journal—a Web log, or "blog" as they are called by Web surfers.

For security purposes I needed a pseudonym on my Web site. The nickname "Wiggles" has followed me off and on since third grade when someone on the playground called me "Pauly-Wolly-Wiggles." Since I was a chief warrant officer (CW), the name "Chief Wiggles" seemed to fit. I titled my Web log, "Chief Wiggles—Straight From Iraq."

Initially, I was getting 10-15 visitors to the site each week—probably just my wife and kids. Then other people started linking to my site and readership began to grow. On a slow news day, when nobody linked to my site, I might have 500 to 800 visitors a day. When major sites linked to my blog, my readership would often exceed 10,000 people. On an average day, over 2,000 would visit.

After sharing some toys with the little girl at the palace gate, I posted a request on my Web site for more toys to replenish my supply and to keep the good work moving forward. I was overwhelmed by the response.

Pretty soon, I was able to turn to my stash of toys any time I had a few spare minutes to head off to a hospital or orphanage as part of my military responsibilities. The toys continued to arrive in my office and I continued to find children who loved receiving them.

One morning, a local orphanage with about 100 girls was having a field day at the Babylon Hotel, not far from the CPA palace. I loaded up some of the toys I had collected into one of the 20-passenger buses which served the palace compound—buses kindly donated by

Children greeting Chief Wiggles in the toy bus.

Saddam Hussein. These buses had been used by Saddam to shuttle government workers around the compound, but they now served the Coalition. I christened the bus, "Chief Wiggles' Toy Bus."

It was a great day as our group of volunteers met with the young Iraqi girls who were on a rare field trip away from the orphanage they called home. They were playing in the garden and tennis court areas of the hotel, when we pulled up with a busload of items carefully selected for them.

They were ecstatic as they saw us walking in carrying boxes of toys, school supplies, and mounds of stuffed animals. You could see the sparkle in their eyes and their grins of anticipation, as each of them greeted our volunteers with a confident, "Hello. What is your name?"

The girls were eager to include us in their games and festivities and grabbed hold of my hands to play their version of ring-around-the-rosy. They sang, chanted, danced, and clapped, but most of all they laughed. It was a full-hearted laugh, indicating at least for that moment, they were completely happy.

After spending a couple of hours with the girls, we made our way back into the Green Zone. The bus was empty, but we were full of joy. It was exactly what we had anticipated when I made the initial request for more toys.

Next I organized a trip with the doctors at our hospital to do a toy drop at the local children's hospital, which had over 300 beds. I continued to plan these events, which we called "Share Joys with Toys," in order to place the toys everyone had sent into the hands of needy kids.

Late one evening, I met with two of our most valuable sources, Karim and Nabil. They had been helpful in locating hidden Iraqi aircraft around the country. They invited a few of us over to the Al-Rasheed Hotel for a late night pool-side dinner party.

They had brought a famous Iraqi fish dish called *masgoof,* made with a fish which looked like carp, caught in the muddy waters of the Tigris River. It was cooked a special way and served up with a variety of onions, vegetables, and seasonings. It was really quite a treat, though I was a bit hesitant at first to eat it, having seen the Tigris River and what flows into it.

It was quite a scene—definitely a Kodak moment—as all of us gathered around the table snatching up the fish with our flatbread in hand, making pigs of ourselves. We were taught the traditional way to eat the fish without utensils, just pinching off a piece of the sweet meat with our two fingers with bread folded in between.

I had grown close to these two men, Karim and Nabil, whom I had met with on several occasions—close enough to engage them in the traditional Iraqi greeting ritual. This involved going cheek to cheek with them starting with the left, then the right, then back to the left cheek, while making a kissing sound each time, similar to what Latino and other cultures do when they greet a close friend. All that hugging and kissing was a little awkward at first, but became more comfortable with time and was a sign of the strong ties and relationships I had built with these people.

We all had a great evening talking about the issues at hand, politics, the old regime, new possibilities, and a variety of other topics. Even though we were at the Al-Rasheed Hotel, well inside the Green Zone, gunfights could be heard all around us throughout the evening. For some reason, it was a busy night for rapid-fire weapons. A few loud explosions were heard, causing all of us to pause our friendly discussion to wonder what might have happened.

I especially appreciated the old love and war stories from Karim and Nabil as they discussed the details of their escapades of years gone by when they were young and foolish. They shared stories of their travels throughout the world, stories of big-busted Polish women who could really handle their liquor and many fun-filled trips to America.

I was surprised to hear one of the men tell us of his wife and child in America, whom he hadn't seen for the past 20 years, since under Saddam's reign he was prohibited from traveling internationally. He had since married again and now had several children with his second wife. He was hoping to be able to travel to the U.S. once more.

Unexpectedly, our grass-roots effort to bring hope to the children of Iraq had blown out the military's mail system with so many boxes

The support of FedEx and their employees was instrumental in getting toys where they were needed.

of toys that they could no longer handle the volume. Each day the mail van would call ahead alerting me that they had another load of boxes for Chief Wiggles.

Then suddenly, our program to "Share Joys with Toys" received a serious setback. The Army APO mail system decided to clamp down, enforcing their policy forbidding goods to be shipped that were intended to be given to another individual. This policy satisfied an elevated security standard and insured that the troops didn't get packages from unknown individuals. I actually received a "cease and desist" order specifically prohibiting more toys being sent to me at the palace. I understood the Army's position, but that meant we needed to find a way to continue the flow of toys.

Thankfully, Matt Evans, a Maryland attorney and reader of my blog, came up with a kick-butt solution enabling us to continue to reach out to the Iraqi kids with bundles of happiness. He set up a non-profit 501(c)(3) organization—Operation Give. Volunteers then secured warehouse space on the East Coast. Toys were sent to the Operation Give warehouse and then shipped by boat in containers to Iraq.

I was so grateful that volunteers in the U.S. had figured out a way to keep the flow of toys moving. There were hundreds of unknown angels who played a part in putting this solution together and who donated money to help pay for the cost of moving the containers to their final destination in Baghdad.

Operation Give had been launched.

Once again our team of Chief Wiggles' workers descended on a children's hospital in Baghdad with arms full of toys. Our caravan pulled up to the front of the hotel accompanied by several doctors from our local military hospital, Iraqi friends, interpreters, reporters from NBC and Associated Press, and our Combat Camera Crew.

After a quick meeting with the hospital administrator, we grabbed a few carts, and proceeded to deliver our cargo of delight to the children in the hospital. We went from room to room, stopping at as many beds as we could to inquire about the child's condition and prognosis, while we personally handed out a toy selected just for them. It was an incredible experience.

As we went down each hall and ward of the hospital, a following grew behind us as the word of our arrival spread like wildfire. Unfortunately, due to the sheer number of people, we were unable to deliver toys to every employee or family member who desired something. We were there to make sure each and every sick child got a toy.

At one point, a father whose daughter was dying from leukemia, confronted me with a plea for medical treatment not toys. With intense emotion he explained his need for a medical solution to his daughter's ailment, which a toy would not cure. My heart ached for him as I put my arm around him. I was sorry to say that I only had toys in my bag of tricks.

A man, who was small in stature but big in courage, came into my office desperately seeking someone to talk to. He was obviously under a great deal of stress and emotionally distraught.

He began to relay to me his story of how his family's house had just been bombed the night prior, for the second time, due to his involvement with Coalition forces. Over the past several months he had continued to provide us with intelligence regarding underground activities around Baghdad, which had resulted in the discovery of several missiles, numerous bad guys, and many caches of weapons.

He started to divulge additional information about the whereabouts of one of our most wanted individuals. I stopped him mid-sentence to inquire of his family's condition, realizing that they had no safe place to live. I told him that the first priority was to find a safe haven for his family.

It was time for the Good Luck Genie to swing into action. I needed to find this man a place to live with his family somewhere in the Green Zone, which was not going to be easy. There were endless rules and restrictions about getting people into the vacated apartments in the area, but I was determined. I knew divine assistance was going to lead the way.

With Renda along, the three of us jumped into my vehicle as I drove around the area. Miraculously, we met the right people, we went to the right places, and we found a nice apartment in a complex where Saddam's intelligence officers used to live. Everything came together just like I knew it would. When the day was over, all I could do was lay in bed staring up at the ceiling and say, "Wow! What a great day!"

The time had finally arrived for my long-awaited reunion with the freed generals from Camp Bucca—a reunion I had been dreaming of and talking about for months. There were at least six of them who lived in Baghdad. We had been calling for a few days to set up this reunion in order to give some of them a stipend and for me to receive their resumes for any future positions.

It was so strange to see them waiting at the front palace gate dressed up in their finest attire rather than prison jumpsuits. It seemed like a dream from another life. They looked good—no, they looked great!

We had a wonderful meeting, talking about so many things that had happened since my departure from Camp Bucca and their arrival back home. We shared many memories from the camp. Surprisingly, we were able to find humor in many of those experiences. I was so glad to hear they were still our advocates and hopeful for a bright future with the help of the U.S.

Two days later, General Hakim and General Matta, came by to pick me up for a dinner engagement. Just as we had promised each other at Camp Bucca, we were finally all having dinner at Hakim's home with his family. I was so excited to meet his family and share an evening with them. The night was everything I dreamed it would be. The food was delicious, the family was delightful, and the evening was perfect. I relished every minute of it.

I gave Hakim's children a couple of stuffed animals, which they immediately snuggled up to. But what the generals gave me, in

General Hakim receiving a medal of honor from Sadam Hussein (face obscured to protect identity).

return, was unbelievable. The two generals gave me their own personal Medals of Honor they had received directly from Saddam Hussein, for heroic acts of courage performed during their military career. They gave me the actual medal with photos of Saddam pinning it on them.

As I read the letter, looked at the pictures, and felt the medal, I was astonished that they would be willing to give up such a treasured service decoration. Suddenly, I realized that they were showing me that they were completely ready for a new Iraq without Saddam Hussein.

The meal was incredible to say the least. We enjoyed the best of Iraqi cuisine: flatbread, biryani, dorma, tabouli, kabobs. I wasn't sure what some of it was, but it was tasty. We topped it off with a light dessert, fruit, then some nice chocolates and a few more drinks. We stayed until it was almost dark. Unsure of how safe it would be to drive around at night, we knew we had to return to the Green Zone before it got too late.

My phone rang early, waking me from a sound sleep. It was my interpreter, Renda, informing me that the Al-Rasheed Hotel had been attacked again. This time the attack was a missile barrage from nearly point-blank range that killed an American colonel and wounded 18 other people. Visiting Deputy Secretary of Defense, Paul Wolfowitz, went scurrying for safety and was unhurt.

I had been there just a few hours earlier for a late-night swim. Renda, an occupant of the hotel, was unharmed. Once again, the security of the Green Zone had been violated. This attack had likely been planned over a two-month period as terrorists had put together an improvised rocket launcher and figured out how to wheel it into the park across the street from the hotel.

Every time I started to feel that things were settling down into some form of normalcy, I was reminded of the stark reality of this place. We were constantly concerned for what might happen at any given moment, knowing we could never let our guard down.

At noon I dashed out the door, as another group of six Camp Bucca generals were scheduled to arrive at the North Gate. As I went through the checkpoint, I noticed out of the corner of my eye that two of our most valuable sources were waiting to see me. I was expecting new information about the location of stockpiles of gold and money. I called up to the office to see if someone else couldn't come down to check Karim and Nabil through the gate.

I ran to the North Gate to welcome the six generals. As with the first group of six, they were all dressed up in their finest apparel. They were clean shaven, except for their mustaches, with fresh haircuts and a noticeably different twinkle in their eyes.

I embraced them one by one expressing my happiness in seeing them as free men. We joked and laughed, and were able to recall a few humorous and lighthearted times at the POW camp.

Other sources had also arrived at the gate mixed in with the group of generals. As I embraced the generals, the others looked in wonderment as if this was the way I greeted all of my sources. I wondered if they, too, were expecting a big hug. Not wanting to leave them out, I complied with their apparent expectation and extended a jubilant greeting and hugs to all at the gate.

In my office, the generals and I chatted about life since their release and reviewed what was now going to happen to them. Lieutenant Colonel Sarna, who was partly responsible for rebuilding the new Iraqi military, spoke to them for about an hour, reviewing a variety of issues and anticipating their questions and concerns.

Realizing that most of those men had driven for hours to arrive in Baghdad for this appointment, I decided it might be a good idea to have lunch together over at the freshly bombed Al-Rasheed Hotel, where there was an Iraqi restaurant with a pretty good selection of indigenous cuisine.

With my interpreter, Renda, I grabbed buddies Karim and Nabil and the six generals, loaded everyone on the Chief Wiggles Toy Bus and headed over to the restaurant. We had a great meal together, with time to reminisce, talk about their families, and look to the future.

On our return trip back to the North Gate I told them to take a couple of toys home to their families, since all of them had small children. I always left a few boxes of toys on the bus for such special occasions. The toys were like icing on the cake, really capping off a

Renda (left) *made strong connections with the children on all of our outings.*

great reunion. We embraced one last time, said our goodbyes, and I wished them well in their new life.

With the generals on their way, I turned my attention to Karim and Nabil. They came to me with quite a find, uncovering the location of numerous Iraqi helicopters hidden prior to the war. I immediately went to work to determine what would be required to recover those in a timely fashion, before they were cannibalized by others looking to make a quick buck.

I had a morning meeting with a group responsible for rebuilding the Iraqi Air Force. One of the agenda items in the meeting was the discussion around bringing General Hakim on board to assist in the rebuilding effort. General Hakim was scheduled to come in for an afternoon interview.

The meeting was quickly sidetracked by one individual's negative attitude about the general, insinuating that perhaps Hakim was not the man for the position in question. This individual claimed to have spoken with a number of peers who were saying uncomplimentary things about General Hakim.

I could see that the individual had his own agenda and perhaps his own people he was hoping to slide into the position. He had left Iraq several years ago, for unknown reasons, but now returned hoping for some sweet position of influence and authority.

I was personally offended by this man's unfounded attack on General Hakim's credibility. I became somewhat emotional and confrontational, requesting the individual bring in his sources for me to interview. I knew better than anyone in the room possibly could, the general's impeccable character. Having interrogated General Hakim completely and thoroughly, doing my own investigation and living with him for many months, I had unshakable confidence in his capability and credibility.

I was not trying to force the issue, presupposing that the general was the only right person for the job. I wanted them to make the right decision, choosing the best man for the job based on substantive qualifications. At the same time I didn't want to see Hakim unfairly judged by some biased report driven by the ulterior motives of an individual who wanted to bring his crony into the position.

I recused myself from the afternoon interview so as not to impose my bias regarding the matter. I had complete confidence in General Hakim's ability to perform. The end result was that the general sailed through the interview, showing them exactly who he was and what he was all about.

The sounds of explosions rocking Baghdad were commonplace, both day and night. Each explosion reminded me not only of the dangers which lurked outside the Green Zone, but of our vulnerability within this ring of security.

I spoke with a fellow who was asleep in the Al-Rasheed Hotel when a rocket-propelled grenade came through his window, slid along the wall lodging in his closet full of clothes but fortunately did not explode. He was one lucky guy with only glass cuts on his face from the shattering mirror. Had it exploded, he surely would have been killed.

For a few days things had been relatively quiet, except for the sound of the occasional barrage of automatic weapon fire, which felt more like background static than anything threatening. I prayed each evening that the night would pass without incident or death.

All of the entranceways to our buildings were guarded by a group of retired Gurkhas from Nepal, known for being some of the best soldiers in the world. They were all very diligent in performing their duties, taking their security jobs seriously. I had found all of them to be courteous and polite. They had taken the time to learn enough English to greet us with the appropriate salutation. I made friends with a number of them that I saw daily and learned how to greet them in Nepali.

As I pulled into the parking lot, the mail truck was waiting for me with another load of about 25 boxes of toys for Operation Give. With some help from Karim and Nabil, we tossed the boxes on to the bus. I was grateful for another load of toys to distribute.

Along the way we decided to engage in a Chief Wiggles activity, picking up people along the side of the road who were in need of a ride. We picked up two Iraqis carrying a propane tank and a mother and her children who had just been to the market. I had my interpreter pass out toys to the kids before letting them off at their stops.

After dinner, I called the Special Forces Team Leader to join us in my office to review some new intelligence regarding the whereabouts of an individual on the Most Wanted List. The raid was planned for the next night, with detailed responsibilities assigned to each person.

It was about 9 PM, the day nearly spent but not over. I was determined to go for a relaxing swim to unwind and decompress from the day's hectic activities. Changing my clothes, I dashed out to the parking lot, where I came upon one of our sources experiencing car trouble, so I paused to help him with his dead battery. Success put a bounce in my step as I went for my swim.

Hope and faith were our best weapons against the constant barrage of negative reports. The media reports of death only showed what was happening on the surface, but they were never able to capture the bigger picture and the inner complexities of our world. Americans could understand body counts and images of destruction. But educating and informing the world about the deep-rooted and centuries-old issues in Iraq and the region was a far more difficult task.

The media shied away from reporting on the multi-layered and complex nature of the region. Perhaps they didn't possess the knowledge and background to understand the situation, or maybe due to time constraints, chose to deliver a more superficial view. Regardless, if the American people were better informed of the intricacies of Iraq, they might have a very different perception of the work being done in Iraq and the expected outcomes.

The bottom line is that Iraq is a multifarious, complicated, and messy environment, one that I just barely understand myself. There are myriad cultural, religious, tribal, political, historical, and geographical elements all intertwined into a complex web, intermixed with threads of mysticism and superstition, spun by greed and a continual thirst for power and survival ignited by Saddam himself.

Chapter Nine

Ramadan

The pace of life slowed down a bit with the start of Ramadan, the holiest season of the Muslim calendar. For Iraqis, observing the sacred month-long holiday meant ritual fasting, praying, and staying away from earthly pleasures, including smoking, from sunrise to sunset. This was difficult for many of our sources who were chain-smokers. I knew that they were coming in a little on-edge and eager for the sun to go down. As night overtook another day in Baghdad, our sources returned to their homes to celebrate with *iftar*, the meal that breaks the fast.

All day long they filled my head full of stories of corruption, murder, deceit, and attacks on Coalition forces. The overload lights finally went off in my head, having been pumped all day with doom and gloom. My negative story meter was way past the maximum level tolerable for any given day. If I heard one more report of dishonesty and scheming I was going to explode.

The final source of the day nearly lit my fuse. Revealing specific information on corruption within the Governing Council, Iraq's interim governing body, he held back on the real meat unless I met his demands for a car, a phone, and payment for his expenses. I was hoping this Iraqi citizen, out of the goodness of his heart and with a desire to serve his country, would offer up the information that might prove to be invaluable. Instead of reporting corruption, his primary concern was personally profiting from the corruption. Obviously, what I hoped for was not going to happen.

Fortunately, my friends, Karim and Nabil, showed up, allowing me to release some pressure as we discussed ways of moving toys around the country. I even found a warehouse in the Green Zone to house all of the toys and supplies we were collecting.

As we were transporting toys to the warehouse, we were able to hand out some to children in the Green Zone, who were often out playing in the streets. I pulled the bus into one of the neighborhoods, stopping at the sight of the first child on the side of the road. Within a few minutes, we had 50 children gathered around the bus as we passed out items through the windows to the outstretched hands of the children below.

The children were climbing all over the bus. Several were able to stand on the tires and put their faces up to the level of my window in the driver's seat. I made them ask politely, saying "please" and "thank you," as I passed out stuffed animals and toys. Patting their heads, pinching their cheeks, and handing out treats was a pleasant diversion from the soul-grinding task of military debriefing.

A few days later, we gathered in the parking lot at our scheduled time, preparing to depart for another outing for "Sharing Joys with Toys." The bus was overflowing with toys; I felt like I was driving Santa's sleigh. Organizing the convoy was critical, with the Chief Wiggles Toy Bus sandwiched between two Humvees for protection. With loaded weapons across our laps, we took off for a handicapped children's hospital, completely unaware of what we were going to find awaiting us.

We made a quick stop by the Green Zone Army hospital to pick up a few doctors, both American and Iraqi. They wanted to share in the experience of passing out toys. As usual, Karim, Nabil, and Ali were there to offer their assistance, having been with us on most of the other toy outings. It was essential to have Iraqis with us that could speak both Arabic and English. Karim brought his teenage daughter along to be part of the team.

As we pulled up to the back gate of the hospital, we discovered it was actually more of a care facility or asylum. The workers and children were busily preparing for our arrival as they washed and swept the area. Some children were already out in their wheelchairs to offer up an enthusiastic welcome and we were greeted warmly by the director of the facility.

It was immediately apparent that things were very difficult for the children at this facility. As I looked through the bus windshield, I noticed one child sitting on the ground with swarms of flies buzzing around her head and face.

We stepped off the bus into the hospital's open courtyard, which had just been hosed down, but we could still smell and see the unsanitary conditions. I had never seen such a run-down place for handicapped children before. Most of the children appeared to be mentally handicapped and suffering from motor-skill impairments.

Over the next hour, we made our way through the rooms full of children and young adults, passing out carefully selected toys, hoping to bring joy to an otherwise neglected group of children. We handed out balls to those that could play with them, along with Tonka trucks and toy cars to boys who immediately began pushing them along the ground. Stuffed animals were given to all the young girls, who snuggled them as tightly as they could.

It was heart wrenching to say the least. All of us were deeply saddened by the tenement-like circumstances. It was difficult, yet rewarding, as the children responded so warmly. However, Karim's daughter had to return to the bus to wait; she simply wasn't able to handle the deplorable conditions.

Doctor Eaman, an Iraqi medical doctor who frequented the hospital, mentioned that conditions had actually improved over the last few months. They had cleaned up the facility and changed the way the children were cared for. It was hard to imagine how awful it must

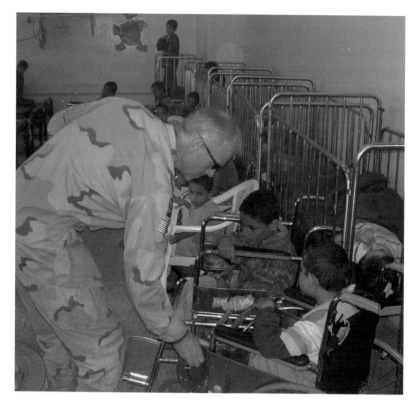

Delivering toys to a care center for severely mentally handicapped children.

have been before the upgrades. They went out of their way to show us a storage room that had been converted into a cafeteria. We were shown another room which had been made into a usable playroom. This enabled the children to be taken out of their rooms during the day. The surroundings were bleak for these forgotten children.

The hospital director was appreciative of our efforts to help these children have a few moments of recreation. She mentioned other such facilities around the country with even worse conditions, which were desperately in need of our assistance. It was painful to think that what she said might be true.

I was aware that, in addition to toys, many Americans had made cash donations on www.operationgive.org. I promised to assist in making some facility improvements and vowed to work with the hospital director in any way I could. I offered to put a padded play mat in the playroom so that the children wouldn't have to play on the cold cement floor.

As we drove away, I thought what a great experience it was and how we had made a difference with something as small and simple as a toy.

My day began with the news of the downing of a Chinook bringing troops from Fallujah back to Baghdad for some R&R. The heavy transport helicopter was hit by two missiles, resulting in 15 soldiers being killed and 26 others wounded.

As the forces of anarchy combined against us, we pushed on knowing that it was going to be some time before we could turn that country back over to its people. Iraqis were just starting to glimpse the responsibility associated with their newfound freedom. I was certain that many citizens didn't fully understand the correlation between freedom and law and order.

Freedom represented a threat to many individuals and factions who were now losing their grip on the minds of the Iraqi citizens. Through the use of terror, these people had been totally manipulated and controlled. The forces of evil benefited enormously, both in money and power, as they perpetuated the bondage imposed upon the people. The enslavement of their minds was finally coming to an end.

Each day I was deluged with a continual flow of information, rumors, stories, hearsay, sightings, and personal experiences concerning the evil side of life in Iraq. Everywhere I turned, I ran head-on into another story of corruption. Illegal and unethical behavior pervaded all aspects of life, with many people consumed by their own desires for money, wealth, power, and importance. There were days I wondered if democracy ever had a chance.

It concerned me as I saw public opinion back home so easily swayed by the media's attempt to promote distaste for this conflict. It was amazing how quickly people's attitudes swung the other direction when we were not able to provide a quick resolution to the problems of Iraq. We were spoiled by the apparent easiness of our military victory over our enemies, not realizing the complexity of the situation we were facing. We were encountering variables that had been in the making for hundreds of years, which we were only beginning to comprehend. As was observed by many, "Winning the war was easy compared to winning the peace."

If anyone should have doubts, it should be the ones being shot at. But American soldiers, in the middle of the conflict, maintained complete confidence in our leaders and continued steadfast in our belief regarding our mission in Iraq. We were the ones at the battlefront doing our part to bring about a speedy and peaceful solution to this conflict. We were firm in our commitment that the world would be better off with a free Iraq.

As I worked away in my office one night, the sound of incoming mortar rounds drove me into the basement of the palace to seek refuge. It wasn't particularly frightening, but the enemy's increasing luck or improving accuracy was a little unnerving. Several of the rounds found cars in the parking lot nearby as their target. Fortunately, no one was hurt as a result of these explosions. But we were all a bit rattled.

The next night, in anticipation of additional incoming rounds and hoping to lighten up the situation, I made a little wager with the guards at the front gate of the palace concerning what time we would hear the incoming rounds that night. Each of us picked a time and threw a couple of bucks into the kitty.

At my selected time I began hearing a string of explosions but realized quickly they weren't incoming but outgoing. It sounded as if we were really stirring up somebody's life. I wasn't exactly sure what it was, but it sounded like tanks and helicopters were involved. It went on for several minutes, one explosion after another. Knowing that we were taking action, I found those sounds of return fire especially encouraging. That was a wager I was happy to lose.

The enemy mortar fire, return fire, and organized enemy attacks continued. One night after returning from appointments, I received a call from one of my sources, who informed me that he could see someone launching mortars in front of his house. He reported that this terrorist was driving up and down the street stopping just long enough to launch a couple of rounds. Hearing that news, I went over to the JOC to inform them of this activity, confident one of the Special Forces teams could stop this one-man rampage immediately.

One night while out at one of the gates, I came across a family trying to get in to visit a family member hospitalized at the Green Zone facility. The guards were not able to allow them entrance, so I agreed to carry in the sack of food they had prepared, after checking the contents thoroughly. I had a couple of stops to make before arriving at the hospital, but finally made it to my destination with the sack of goodies, only to find that the patient had been transferred to another hospital outside of my area. I left the sack anyway, hoping the hospital might be able to send the food over with another runner.

It was the continual newness of life in Iraq, the constant change brought about by the evolution of variables in and out of my control, which kept my time there so exciting and meaningful. Everything was in a state of flux; there was no such thing as status quo.

Each day's unpredictability made waking in the morning such a treat. Change was the only constant. I woke each day without any idea of what might happen or what new thing might fall into my lap.

In the course of my discussions with numerous sources, I continued to hear the word *jinn*, or genie, brought up as Iraqis discussed the supernatural powers of Saddam and his followers. Even the most educated of Iraqi sources, which I would have expected to be more sensible, believed in the powers of the genie tribes. Their belief system acknowledged a separate realm, or spirit world, referred to as the "genie world" which consisted of different colored genie tribes. Saddam was supposedly in charge of the Red Genie Tribe and, as their master, he could command the forces of the genies as he willed.

Out of curiosity for what was behind this belief, I began to ask sources if they had ever seen or had any dealings with a genie. I was surprised by the answers I received and the extent of their belief in the world of the genies, which are described in the Quran as "spirits of evil."

There were so many supposed eye-witness accounts and genie sightings that I began having them describe what they saw, while our artist/interpreter listened and illustrated what they said. I ended up with quite a collection of stories and drawings of monster-like creatures, half human and half animal, with mixed animal parts.

One day, Yousef, one of our sources, brought with him a man who claimed to be the Green Genie Tribe Master. Yousef said he was going to use the Green Genie Tribe Master to help us find Saddam Hussein. As he closed the drapes of the room and laid down enough cardboard for all of us to sit down, he motioned for us to take off our shoes and sit in a circle.

For what seemed like an eternity, we sat listening to the Genie Master's understudy acting as the medium for the genies to speak to us. He spoke using a different voice as if the genie were speaking through him. After listening to all kinds of gibberish and strange tales of seemingly inconceivable things, we couldn't help but be somewhat skeptical, at times we had to work to hold back laughter.

Then, all of a sudden, the Genie Master jumped to his feet while informing us that the Red Genies were coming and they needed to leave the building immediately. Within a few seconds all of them were standing, had put their shoes on, and were running down the corridors of the palace in an attempt to get to their cars before the genies arrived.

It was quite a sight to behold—grown men in suits running for their lives from these invisible but powerful genies. That was the last time we heard from the Genie Master and nothing ever came of any of the marvelous insights gleaned from the Genie Master's séance.

With the fall of Saddam came the revamping of a weak and corrupt judicial system. One of our sources brought in a judge who had just been brought before a board of review in the Ministry of Justice. The board was questioning his past behavior under Saddam. The judge feared that, having spent 25 years working under Saddam's judicial system, he might not have a future in the new system. They had come to me in hopes of getting some help in securing his position, since many of the Saddam-era judges had been dismissed. I had an opportunity to give this man his own day of reckoning for what he had done.

He was obviously very nervous, beads of sweat were running down his forehead as he squirmed uncontrollably in his seat. I believed he knew his previous behavior was questionable and that his position as a judge was in jeopardy. He was an older man, well into his 60s, nicely dressed in a suit and tie, prepared with a thick file of references from other judges who had written statements regarding his integrity.

It was my chance to get up on my soapbox to discuss with him my perspective on the relationship between liberty and law, and the responsibilities of the judicial system. I was on a roll and things were really flowing. This guy was starting to twitch.

I told him that regardless of what the rules were before, there was a new sheriff in town with a new system, one dependent on high-level people living up to a higher standard. For this new system to work, judges and attorneys alike needed to be the examples of obedience to the law, unapproachable by the criminal element of their society. The system itself was dependent on the honesty and integrity of the people put in positions to enforce the law. Judges would now set the bar for what would be expected of the citizens of Iraq.

If judges of the past regime indulged in corruption and bribery, then we had to assume that they would continue to do so under the new system. Anyone tied to the criminals of the past needed to be weeded out, even if that meant that we completely cleaned house. So far over 100 judges had been released for their participation in corrupt activities.

I admonished him that the judicial system had to be secure in its position to enforce the law, fairly and justly dishing out punishments to those convicted of crimes. If, for whatever reason, the judges of the land did not respect the law, breaking it whenever it suited their needs, then the land would continue to be anarchic and full of citizens who would not abide by the law. There had to be a changing of the guard if the current judicial system was no longer able to secure the rights of the people under the law.

I told him that judges who had committed crimes should come forward before they were prosecuted, to discuss their crimes, and cooperate with us in prosecuting others who were also involved.

Then I gave him an ultimatum. He had one chance to come clean with the details of his past, exposing his own involvement in shady or questionable activities. I was only going to ask him once for information regarding himself and his colleagues. I was asking him to report others who were also involved in corruption at his level.

I asked this judge to write up a report discussing everything he knew about corruption in the judicial system, with names and activities including his own. I told him I wanted it on my desk in one week, this being the only time I would discuss this matter with him.

He fidgeted around offering up reasons and excuses for his fellow judges, of course being careful not to implicate himself in any way. He continued to speak of other judges and their problems, as if to say he was not involved. Depending on what he reported, I intended to fully interrogate him about his own activities once he returned, especially if he was not divulging the truth about his own involvement. I was really having a good time running this approach on him, hoping to reap some good details when finished.

Work in the CPA palace, especially in our office, was a hectic, unpredictable, bizarre pressure cooker. But there were also moments, usually late in the evening, where the palace had a satisfying, collegial, and almost sacred atmosphere. Each day was something new.

My trailer was a stone's throw from the palace back door, just a minute's walk away. That's what I call a nice commute. The palace was home to Ambassador Bremer, as well as dozens of ministers, generals, envoys, and dignitaries. Add to this number, the thousands of Coalition support staff, both Iraqi and American personnel, and you have a small city.

Security was tight and days were long. I was up by 6 AM every morning to get ready for the day. I would usually arrive at the office by 7:30 AM, putting in 12- to 14-hour days, plus a working lunch or dinner. We would typically meet with sources until 9 PM. After that, we would spend what strength we had left catching up, writing reports, or preparing for the next day's lineup of curious characters.

There was never a day off, except for Christmas and New Year's Day. We worked seven days a week. Friday, the Muslim holy day, was a bit slower—but we were there at the palace cranking out intelligence reports just the same.

All of our meals were served in the dining hall of the palace. This was no ordinary mess hall. It was the size of a large hotel ballroom with marble floors, high ceilings, ornately decorated walls, and chandeliers to match. It seemed odd to be eating meals in this elegantly appointed room that probably once hosted Saddam's most vile insiders. My dusty army boots looked peculiar stomping across the polished marble floors.

In this monstrous and magnificent dining room, equipped to feed 3,000 people three meals a day, the predictable smells and tastes became increasingly monotonous but were still more welcome than MREs. There were no set meal times for us as we were forced to catch a bite whenever we could find time. Long lines in the cafeteria-style hall made it frustrating at times but gave us a chance to chitchat with others working in the palace. It was a good break from the grind of the day for our team to grab a bite while laughing about the events of the day. There was usually a nice salad bar and several typical American entrée choices, plus a few side dishes and desserts—nothing that would make it into a gourmet cookbook, but there was plenty to eat. Once in a while we would even have the option of eating some delicious curry dishes prepared by our cooks from India.

The convenience and safety of the palace made it easy for us to bring our sources and contacts to the dining hall to build relationships over a meal. Of course, we had to be careful to not wander into classified or sensitive topics in such a public venue. Many sources refused to be seen going into the palace and would insist that we meet more discreetly off-site in one of the numerous small cafes in the Green Zone.

At the end of the day, we were often so keyed-up that we knew sleep would be impossible. To break the tension, we would frequently go dancing at the Al-Rasheed Hotel. The Al-Rasheed was about two miles from the palace, an easy walk and an even shorter drive. There was a favorite nightclub at the hotel with a DJ who played a good variety of popular American tunes from the '70s on. The DJ would occasionally toss in some Iraqi pop music for the native Iraqis working in the Green Zone. That music was a little difficult to dance to at first, but I eventually got the hang of it after several dance lessons from Renda. Dancing started around 10 PM each night just as Baghdaddy, Renda, and I were arriving. Since the men outnumbered the women about ten to one, we would often go just for the music, snacks, and sodas. But sometimes I would toss social customs to the wind and dance by myself for the exercise and emotional release it provided, while Baghdaddy looked on sipping a Coke. He wasn't much for dancing.

Many nights, after the sources had been sent home, we contemplated the events of the day wondering how we got it all done. We were often too exhausted to go anywhere, so we would just hang together at the palace. In the privacy of our oversized office, we would crank up the boom box, share goodies from home, and sing at the top of our lungs. I am sure that passersby saw our shadows dancing around through the office window and wondered what was going on. It was a nice way to unwind from a day that was chaotic and stressful.

Sometimes, just for the fun of it, I would play Master Chef and we'd cook up a few delectable dishes, the likes of which you'd never find in the mess hall. The creativity of working with strange and unfamiliar local ingredients increased the challenge. My wife would sometimes send me interesting curries or spices that would spark a culinary spree. I would go to the market and buy fresh produce— tomatoes, onions, garlic, whatever else caught my eye—and return to make some tasty dish like chicken curry or zesty spaghetti, a nice upgrade from our normal fare. Sometimes we were just hungry for a taste of home—like a big stack of homemade pancakes drenched in syrup. The team would usually pitch in on the cooking and clean-up, making the evening fun, delicious, and relaxing.

The only other relief from the daily stress came from planning and executing our toy deliveries for Operation Give. A new ship-ment of cuddly stuffed animals could resuscitate the most miser-able problem-choked day. Receiving a phone call from the mail van announcing a delivery from the States would brighten up the day for all of us. With minimal resources we developed an incredibly effi-cient system. Whichever team member was available would receive

Specialist Conan "Baghdaddy" Heimdal makes friends with an Iraqi boy during a toy delivery.

the shipment, transfer the boxes from the mail van to the toy bus, then move the toys directly to the warehouse. Minimum effort and maximum result.

Initially, it was just Chief Allen and me on this elite team of military debriefers. About a month later, we were joined by Specialist "Bagh-daddy" Heimdal, a friend from days at Camp Udairi. The final addition was Sergeant Charm. The four of us constituted the only team of its kind in the palace. If you were an Iraqi with some important information to share with the Coalition—if you knew the where-abouts of weapons, bombs, insurgents, land mines, money, or persons of interest, and wanted to give that information to the highest level in the country—we were your first line of contact.

With such a critical mission, it was important for members of our team to stay well connected with each other. Although we had separate vehicles and were often spread out on assignments all over the area, we were in constant contact with each other, particularly by cell phone. For both security and success we had to work closely together. We learned to play to each others' strengths and cover each others' weaknesses.

Each team member brought different skills and abilities that we weaved into a system that worked well and kept us going day after day. Chief Allen was particularly good working with tribal leaders and in working with Russell, one of our expert interpreters. Debriefing tribal leaders required the ability to work effectively with competing factions and the complex politics of these groups. Chief Allen and Russell were well-versed in the U.S. strategies in dealing with these men and their bickering contingents. As the third man, Baghdaddy often was forced to play "clean up," handling the most obnoxious or annoying sources who were just looking for a job, money, or some other favor. Sergeant Charm, the new kid on the block, rounded out the team with his remarkable sense of humor and edgy originality. Laughter became the super-glue for our team.

Some sources just dropped in at one of the Green Zone gates throughout the day, while others were brought in by nationals working in the palace. There was no telling, at any given time, how many sources we would be dealing with and there was no way to schedule or manage the flow. Dealing with such a high volume of Iraqi sources, all with unfamiliar and seemingly similar names, we were forced to come up with creative ways to keep them all straight. We gave many of them code names, partly for confidentiality and partly to bring some fun to this intense kind of work. There was "Fat Tony," "The Snake Charmer," "Stinkypants," and many others. We even had an in-house caricaturist who would draw spontaneous cartoons poking fun at some of the more bizarre characters.

No question about it, we were loose cannons—but only in a good sense. To a certain degree, we ran our own show and we had free rein. We were given a clearly defined mission, then cut a wide berth in what we could do, say, offer, and promise to sources. Our commanding officers weren't in our building nor did we have daily contact with them. With this kind of relaxed leadership, we became experts at instant improvising, creative problem-solving, and devising off-the-wall workable solutions to our daily dilemmas—while not having to get approval for every move like some rookie salesman on a used car lot.

Strangely, many of the people working at the CPA palace could spend their entire tour there and never meet an Iraqi face to face. It was secluded, well-guarded, and highly secure—a totally American compound in the heart of Baghdad, with more acreage than Central Park.

In contrast, the nature of our position put us in continuous daily interaction with Iraqis at every level of the social, professional, political, and military hierarchy. Learning how to effectively deal with them and gain their trust was our constant challenge.

There was always a lot going on in our office, demanding different resources, different strategies, and different skills. We were family that looked out for and took care of each other. To remain successful, safe, and sane we were always watching each others' backs, filling in for each other, and pulling up the slack from time to time. We were tightly bound together by an unspoken creed.

Our team interacted at the highest level of Coalition operations, working with officials, military brass, and ministries every day. We all knew what our mission was and we jumped in with both feet to make it happen. We moved as fast as we could with an uncanny ability to coordinate the demands of a pretty messy environment. To many outsiders it probably appeared that we were operating out of control. But this is what it took to accomplish our task. When anyone entered our domain and attempted to make sense of it all, they would usually give up.

At any given moment you could find us running in a dozen different directions yet remaining cohesive and focused at the same time. We wouldn't have had it any other way. We loved each other like brothers, giving full confidence to each individual on the team. There was no doubt, no mistrust, and no confusion. We were one in purpose. We were a team.

Once again I was behind the wheel of the Chief Wiggles Toy Bus. This time I was in an area of the Green Zone where I hadn't spent much time. I pulled the bus up to the side of the road as I saw a few kids playing in a pile of rubble behind some bombed out buildings. I had a few toys in the back, as I usually did, in anticipation of seeing children. Renda knew what was going on as she quickly dashed to the back of the bus to grab a few stuffed animals. She was the first one out of the bus handing out the stuffed animals to the little girls that had gathered. Seeing a couple of boys, I went back to snag a few toy cars for them.

These kids were extremely poor, with their shredded and stained clothes and shoeless feet. Their skin was cracked from the extremes of the weather, their faces dirty from not bathing, their hair tangled and stringy, and the only toys in sight were the broken bricks of the demolished building they were playing in.

Pulling the toy cars from behind my back where I had hidden them, I handed one to the littlest boy in the group. As he looked down at the toy car in his hands, his eyes opened as big as two silver dollars and his mouth dropped wide open. Then a huge smile came across his whole face, responding as if he had never held a toy before.

No words were spoken or necessary; his face fully expressed his appreciation for the moment. My only regret was that I didn't have my camera to capture it. Those expressions of joy never became routine or commonplace. Each new experience was exciting, fresh, and totally satisfying.

Mopping up from a war meant living on a continual roller coaster of emotions from one moment to the next, as we dealt with the constant flow of intelligence regarding the activities of our enemies beyond the walls of the Green Zone. We continued to be bombarded with information regarding the very worst that mankind had to offer in a quest for power, money, position, revenge, and every other evil desire.

A visible and tangible struggle of good versus evil persisted on a daily basis. Through Saddam's chains of bondage, evil had a stranglehold on the minds of the Iraqi people for decades. Over the years,

Saddam established an entwining of culture, tradition, tribal mentality, and religion, to create a society of hatred, revenge, greed, and distrust. He made every effort to control all aspects of their lives, keeping them in the dark about so many things, force-feeding them a continual flow of misinformation that brainwashed them completely.

At one time or another, many of these people had been tortured, imprisoned, beaten or punished for a variety of seemingly minor infractions. Almost without exception, the sources we spoke with had the scars to prove the stories of such abuse. We had almost become numbed by the endless stream of stories relating to the enslavement, abuse, and torture of these people.

For the most part they had been fed so much misinformation regarding the U.S. and the rest of the world that they still distrusted our actions and feared our intentions. They had been told, for example, that we were there to steal their oil. Many believed that we were there to take their money, exploit their resources, occupy their country, and abuse the Iraqi people.

Our enemies were using a blasphemous blend of religion, government, and culture to exploit their cause, calling for more hatred, more distrust, more revenge, and more resistance. Their whole purpose was driven by a lust for power and money.

Our enemies existed both externally and internally, everywhere that people sought to satisfy their own greedy desires for wealth, position, and control. It was a disease that spread like wildfire, fueled by the actions of those at the highest levels of that society—in the Iraqi police department, judicial system, and the Governing Council.

As the facts streamed in regarding corruption at the highest levels, I felt the pain of those people who did not seem to be able to break free of the grip of Saddam. The stories, the lies, the crimes, and the atrocities weighed me down at times.

I had some cases involving many of the new people we put in power at the highest levels, within the very organizations responsible for enforcing the law and setting a new standard. Increasingly, we encountered episode after episode of new leaders taking advantage of their positions to exploit and abuse their own people. The well-established patterns of the old regime were trying to resurface.

A steady stream of sources had firsthand knowledge of corruption within the new government. I was building a large file against several individuals that had lied about their background, their involvement with the old regime, their previous positions and ranks, and continued to spin a web of deceit and lies.

I maintained a strong hope for the people of Iraq; I loved many of them dearly. It was devastating to see the future of Iraq jeopardized by a few selfish and egotistical individuals.

Most of the Iraqi people saw and felt the goodness of Americans, which was evident in all that we did—the way we interacted with them, the way we went out of our way to avoid hurting innocent civilians, the way we responded with compassion, and the way we believed in them.

Our sources continued to come to our office bearing gifts to show their appreciation for our presence and express their gratitude for what we had done for them. Some of them had expressed a desire to have us over for dinner once Ramadan ended. They wanted to share their jubilation as they celebrated Saddam's removal; they were full of hope for what lie ahead.

As Ramadan came to an end, the fasting gave way to feasting. Eid is a three-day holiday of feasting and gift-giving at the conclusion of Ramadan. During this time it's customary for families to travel around to friends and relatives, sharing meals and giving gifts.

If someone drops in with their children during Eid, you're expected to have gifts, money, or both for the little ones. Several of our important sources brought their children over to meet me, which

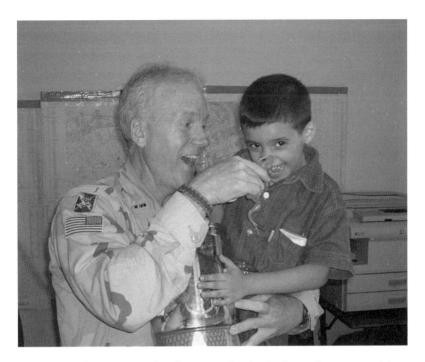

There were always toys on hand to entertain the children who came to visit at the CPA.

gave me an opportunity to give toys from America to the children and to solidify our relationship with their parents.

I got a call from the North Gate from a source named Mohammed. He had come with his kids to introduce them to me. I was happy to oblige. As I slipped out the door, I quickly made a stop at the warehouse to pick up a few toys. He had a beautiful young daughter and cute twin boys.

I put together a small box of school supplies, stuffed animals, small toy cars, and special items I thought each would like, with a couple of new toothbrushes and toothpaste to top it off. I pulled up in the toy bus and motioned for them to jump in, as Mohammed gathered the kids and pushed them inside. I drove over to a quiet spot out of traffic.

The children were quiet, not really sure about how to act around an American, especially an American soldier with full army gear and a loaded weapon in his lap. They were all dressed up in their finest clothes, nicely groomed, obviously cleaned up for the occasion. They were beautiful kids, evidently taking after their mother, who wasn't able to make the trip.

I placed the box on my lap and took out each item, handing them to the intended child, whose eyes opened wide in anticipation. They were appreciative and well-mannered as they offered up a sincere, "Thank you very much," in Arabic.

I first met Mohammed a couple months prior under very different circumstances. He appeared at the North Gate and told the guards that he had some valuable information which he desired to pass along to someone. I took the call and told the guard I would be out at the gate to pick him up momentarily.

When I arrived at the gate with an interpreter, I saw Mohammed, a tall, skinny, Iraqi man in his late 30s. He seemed somewhat nervous and uneasy. I broke the ice by introducing myself as the CPA's debriefer and told him I would be more than happy to speak with him about his information.

He was comparatively well dressed, in a suit and tie, which struck me as odd considering the attire worn by most of my sources. He was clean-cut and freshly shaven. He spoke a small amount of English, attempting to initially talk to me on his own without the use of my interpreter. He seemed unsure about what he was doing, but pressed on nonetheless.

In his quiet humble way, he told me about a number of illegal activities he had witnessed firsthand, but the one thing that stuck out in my mind was his story about a counterfeiting operation going on in Baghdad. He seemed to have explicit details about this operation, saying that he used to work for the man who was in charge. He knew everything about what, where, when, and how this counterfeiting ring had been and was operating.

After having worked as a debriefer for only a couple of months I had already become quite cynical. I was getting tired of listening to so many rumors of operations and activities that never panned out. But this one seemed different. The amount of detail was surprising, giving him significant credibility. He claimed to have been there and seen the operation with his own eyes. He drew me a map of the area, named the streets, and gave me the layout of the counterfeiters' premises.

I told him our next step was to get one of our action teams, a Special Forces team, to go out with him to scope out the area. I asked him if he would be willing to travel with the team to identify the location and the specific buildings involved. He said he would, but only if we provided some type of cover or disguise.

The next couple of months were ultimate frustration as I tried to entice any of our teams to pick up the lead and make the initial recon of the area, in hopes that they would then conduct the raid and take down the criminals. To my dismay and disappointment, I could not get any takers. Even after discussing the details with various groups, I was turned down flatly each time with the excuse that they were too busy or were focusing on more important targets.

After each attempt to persuade someone to take the bait and turn Mohammed's information to action, my source became more and more discouraged with my lack of results, wishing at times that he had not come forward with the information. He had taken a great amount of risk in coming to talk to me, especially since he was quite close to the kingpin. He was concerned about his wife and small children, knowing that we would not be able to protect him from any retaliation.

I finally realized I was not going to be able to facilitate any type of action against these criminals through normal channels and decided

I needed to take another course of action. After serious reflection on the matter, I decided to hand the case over to a team of policemen from Hella, a suburb of Baghdad, who were working with the Governing Council. I had worked with the Hella police chief for some time and knew his allegiance to our cause. I set up an appointment to introduce Mohammed and his evidence to this group to take action.

They did their initial drive-by to survey the area, came up with a game plan, and selected a day for it to go down. Everything seemed ready to go, with the Hella police ready for any and all contingencies, or so it seemed.

On the night of the scheduled raid, the Hella policemen conducted their surprise attack on the counterfeiting gang at the designated location just as planned. But they did not expect the Baghdad police to show up at the appointed time to supposedly assist in the operation. Once the doors were opened and several hundred satellite dishes were discovered on the scene, the Baghdad police were so busy trying to steal or hide the dishes for themselves that the whole operation became chaotic, unruly, and was nearly a disaster.

The leader of the Hella policemen frantically called me that night in my office to see if I couldn't solicit the help of the American MPs in the vicinity to secure the area. I immediately complied with his request, mainly to prevent the Baghdad policemen from stealing the evidence. With the help of the MPs in the immediate vicinity, several criminals were arrested, bags and bags of evidence were confiscated, and the printing presses were destroyed. They seized the plates, negatives, and the equivalent of several million dollars in Iraqi counterfeit currency.

Surprisingly, the counterfeiting operation was producing both the old and the new Iraqi currency, suggesting that the operation had been up and running long before the start of the war. We were also surprised that the operation was producing the new currency at least two weeks before it was to be officially released for distribution in Iraq. There was also evidence at the scene which led us to believe

Printing presses used by the counterfeiters.

that the operation had connections to Saddam's sons and links to organizations in other countries.

The bust had been a very successful operation and a triumph for all those involved. All the evidence was taken the next day over to the Iraqi Governing Council to be put on display and filmed by several news crews. This was big news and made the headlines of the morning paper.

But the real story was what transpired next. After the criminals had been in jail in Hella for a week or so, they were inexplicably transferred over to the Karada police station in Baghdad. We then heard stories from policemen at that station that a police division head, Chief Jamal, had his driver showing up on a daily basis with food and comfort items for the prisoners.

Within a matter of days after they had been jailed in Baghdad, the prisoners were, to our total disappointment, released by the judge and the policemen at that station. I was outraged, feeling

An Iraqi counterfeiter is captured with a box of phony bills in the lower foreground.

discouraged for trying to make a difference only to be thwarted by the police and the judge. No sooner did we get the counterfeiters behind bars, than they were released by a corrupt system that was supposed to be upholding and enforcing the law.

At that point I was determined to get to the bottom of this case, to find out who was involved in the counterfeiters' release and why. I began gathering information about the policemen at the Karada station and about the judge who allowed them to flee. At every turn it became evident that the police and the judge had been paid off. All the evidence led back to Chief Jamal.

Once the word got out at the CPA that I was working on the corruption of the police and the judicial system, then other people at the CPA, from the Ministry of Interior, their own internal affairs staff, and the Ministry of Justice, began coming to my office to collaborate with me on this case. They had also started their own investigation of the police and the Ministry of Justice to uncover and eliminate any type of corruption in the ranks of the judicial and law enforcement systems.

We began having regular meetings to share information and to coordinate our efforts to determine the scope and depth of the problem. Both the Ministry of Interior and the Ministry of Justice began turning over sources to me for debriefing, individuals who claimed to have had firsthand knowledge of corrupt activities being conducted by the police. I personally met with numerous sources who were victimized by the Iraqi police. Case after case cited the mismanagement of evidence, theft, corruption, and bribery, all of which seemed to lead to the top and to Chief Jamal.

I was beginning to have quite a large file on their corrupt activities, even getting direct information from former policemen who were aware of the workings of the police department. One former policeman brought me several citizens who had been victimized, relating to me independently the sad details of their encounter with the police.

One evening I was taken by the head of the Iraqi Internal Affairs department over to the home of the Iraqi Minister of Interior to have a late night discussion. The Minister informed me of a vote that was going to be taking place the next morning by the Governing Council to elect Chief Jamal to the position of deputy minister, further empowering him with more control and additional potential for corruption.

As I heard about this election, I felt I needed to do whatever I could to make key persons aware of the case I had been building against Chief Jamal. I felt an urgency to inform those in positions of power and control to consider the evidence against him, before making their decision. My heart and my mind compelled me to act, to do something, to make others aware of the potential dangers of the Governing Council's impending actions.

With the words of the Minister still ringing in my head, I raced back to my office to write several letters to Ambassador Bremer's office, to the Governing Council, and to my own chain of command, to make sure they all knew what was going on. I sent emails to those in command so they would know what I'd done and be able to act promptly. This was serious. Something needed to happen immediately.

About 7:45 AM, before there was much activity in the compound, I discreetly dropped off a letter to the ambassador and to the Governing Council outlining the information that I had collected, hoping for a speedy response to this potentially inflammatory intelligence.

Almost immediately, I received a call from Ambassador Bremer's office. Instead of interest in the issues I was presenting, I was peppered with questions regarding the whereabouts of the letter I had written to the Governing Council. The executive assistant to the ambassador did not hide her irritation in her sharp command.

"Retrieve it immediately."

I wanted to explain my position, to discuss the situation, to consider options, but this was the Army. I heard myself snap an immediate, "Yes, ma'am," as I jumped into action.

Fortunately, I knew exactly where I had placed the letter that morning. It was clearly addressed to the head of the Governing Council, Adnan Pachachi, placed in a manila folder, and prominently left for his scheduled arrival. But over half an hour had passed and I started to panic thinking that maybe it had already been opened. If so, I was doomed.

Dashing back to the Governing Council's office, I held my breath as I turned the corner. The meeting the letter was intended for was scheduled to start in a few minutes. Surely, it would be gone.

But there it was. Still in its place, in the folder where I had left it, seemingly untouched. I snatched it quickly and darted back to my office. I arrived trembling, but grateful.

I never did hear back from anyone in my chain of command regarding the contents of the letter, leaving me somewhat dismayed by the whole experience. I had been told that my mission was to gather information of a critical nature and push it to action in a timely fashion. I was unable to do so in this case, watching it end suddenly and without results.

No one in the ambassador's office ever explained what I did wrong or what they were concerned about, but the letter hung over me like a dark cloud for the remainder of my tour in Iraq.

In the course of further investigation, I discovered that the judge had released the prisoners due to "lack of evidence," even though the judge himself had signed a receipt for the very evidence he was claiming did not exist. I saw the receipt and a list of the evidence that was turned in at the time of the counterfeiting operation raid. It was clear that the judge had been paid off or blackmailed to ignore the evidence.

The judge was later removed from office after I turned the file over to the Ministry of Justice.

One afternoon, our team went to the Green Zone Community Center which housed a girls' primary school—another episode in the "Share Joys with Toys" campaign. We passed out toys and school supplies, all made possible by generous people from the other side of the world. It was always the high point of the week, getting out into the community, sharing the bounty of so much kindness.

For the most part, the abandoned homes of the former regime employees in the Green Zone were left in pretty bad condition after having been destroyed or totally ransacked of every possible thing of value. Many of the families who moved into the area were destitute and little more than squatters in the neighborhood.

The school itself was totally run-down, having been neglected for years. Education was not a priority for Saddam's repressive regime. The poorly lit school room was an eyesore: paint peeling, desks cracked, chairs dilapidated, and walls barren. There was absolutely nothing fun or interesting that you would expect in an elementary school.

But the kids were great. The young ladies were so well behaved and well mannered, all sitting patiently in their chairs, quick to respond in unison with a loud, rehearsed, "Good morning," in English. They looked beautiful, with smiles that were tempered with a certain shyness typical of Iraqi girls who are hesitant to respond even when prompted to do so.

We went from room to room with boxes of toys, making sure that everyone received something to brighten their day. We passed out combs and hairbrushes, pencils and pens, dolls and stuffed animals. The gifts were ideal for these girls, appreciation beaming from their faces.

We sat down with them in their little chairs and desks. It was a tight fit, but it made them laugh. I bumbled my way through a few words I had learned in Arabic. It was great to hear their laughter and to see their smiles.

I saved a few of the best toys for last, not sure how to give out a few special items to a classroom of girls. I decided to have a little quiz to see who was keeping up on current events. I stood in front of the class with my interpreter and instructed them to raise their hand if they knew the answer. I requested they not blurt out the answer and told them we would select the first hand raised.

I asked, "Who is the President of the United States?" They all blurted out, "Bush." With no way to select a winner for that round, I had to go with more difficult questions like, "What is the capital of the U.S.?" and "What is the population of Iraq?"

As their little hands quickly popped up, the first hand was chosen and the special toys were handed out to the delighted winners. It was a great experience for the team and the news crew that had tagged along.

It was strange to be in an elementary school, a place for young kids to learn, with no colored pictures on the walls but plenty of graphic depictions of war and the military. Weapons and soldiers decorated their walls, giving a twisted idea of what children that age should be learning. It was appalling to see the remnants of the old regime still casting its shadow on the educational system. One dramatic change—Saddam's picture, once in the front of every book, was now noticeably missing from most books.

It was a day of emergencies, each one as important as the next, urgent situations stemming from the of corruption that had already crept into several of the new government organizations. There seemed to be no end to the Saddam wannabes in this country, making the selection process that much more difficult and critical.

One of my sources discovered, defused, and brought to me two bombs planted under bridges outside of Baghdad. They were intended to kill American troops traveling through the area. As a result of this type of information, we were making significant progress: people arrested, weapons found, bombs defused, groups broken up, and attacks prevented.

It was just past midnight, 12:23 AM to be exact. I had just laid down on my bed, grateful for being able to retire at a reasonable hour for a change, when the sound of a screaming mortar round and then the explosion was heard right near our trailer. My trailer buddy and I immediately sat up in bed looking over at each other anticipating additional rounds. Another one was heard which was way too close for comfort. But it was the silence afterwards that was a little unsettling as we listened for additional explosions.

Then came the sound of helicopters, the customary sound of automatic weapon fire and a few retaliatory explosions, signaling that the assailants were on the run. The CPA siren blasted, "Take cover! Take cover! This is not a test." We never doubted it was the real thing. We had been instructed to stay in our trailers and to take cover under the mattress of our beds, rather than running around trying to find more solid protection.

When the all clear signal came, we returned to our beds. But my mind was still engaged in the emergencies of the day rather than the mortar explosions of the night. I had spent most of the week trying to keep my sources alive and out of jail. I had been building a file of information and evidence against several high-ranking officials in the Iraqi police department that I hoped would expose their trail of deceit and corruption. I was grouping our forces as I built my case against them, calling upon all the powers at hand to expedite their removal.

Greed had captured the hearts of so many, greed for money and power. We were continually fighting the battle of weeding out individuals who were trying to take advantage of the situation that existed, with so much money floating around and so many new opportunities to snatch it. Each corrupt individual seemed to be like an octopus attaching a tentacle to anything within his reach, each one creating their own mini-network of corruption.

It was survival of the greediest, everyone grabbing as much as they could for themselves. There was no black and white, only a large gray area between what was thought to be right and wrong, with many people feeling like something was owed them for the years of suffering under Saddam's rule. There was a sense that everyone should take something while there was still something to take.

Sometimes the tables were turned so that the criminals went after the good guys with charges and accusations, putting them on the defensive with fabricated stories. It was difficult to know what the truth of the matter was, not sure whose story to believe. With the counterfeiting gang, once they were released, they turned the charges back against our source, with the help of their crooked judge who issued a warrant for his arrest. They fabricated a story that he had broken into one of their homes and stolen several pieces of jewelry.

There was dishonesty, fraud, and corruption at the highest levels, touching every aspect of life there. The higher it went up through the government, the more difficult it was to terminate, with individual power bases growing and support widening. At times I ran up against people who had become so powerful that others in investigative organizations felt too small to tackle them. That was certainly the case with the top-ranking police officers at the police department; even Internal Affairs was afraid to go after them, fearing they or their families might be killed. It was difficult to see a solution in sight.

Sporadic explosions continued to remind us that we were still in Baghdad, still in a war zone. Even though things seemed to be getting better, with lulls in the action extending for several days, Iraq was still a nation plagued with evil. Fortunately, our team of debriefers was unified in our desire to continue what we had started.

With a warehouse full of toys, it was time for another adventure in sharing. This time we traveled with Ali, Azad, and Renda up north to a small city north of Arbil called Salahuddin, right in the middle

The inventory of toys eventually outgrew the CPA office and were moved to a nearby warehouse.

of the Kurdish region. It was about four hours north of Baghdad. We went in two vehicles, Ali's truck and Azad's Volvo. We filled Ali's pickup truck with boxes of toys and took off.

We met with the mayor of the small town who was expecting us. He had arranged for the neediest families in the village to gather the next morning with their children outside city hall to receive the goodies we had prepared for them. We were expecting about 40 families to show up, but it turned out to be more like 400 once word got out. They had entirely surrounded the building with children of all ages waiting for toys.

The Kurdish media was there to capture the moment. They certainly didn't expect to see this many people, all pressing forward, pushing up against the building. At one point the kids began pounding on the windows of the city hall in hopes that we would pass out toys through the windows. The Kurdish media later broadcast the episode to all the Kurdish satellite channels throughout the world.

Logistics became a problem as we tried to figure out how we were going to expedite the distribution of one toy to each child, insuring that none made their way back in line to pick up another. Just getting all of them to line up in single file was a major undertaking. Getting them to then file through the door in an orderly fashion was easier said than done, with each child wanting to be at the front of the line for better selection.

All in all, it went really well, aside from an occasional burst of frustration or anger from the adults inside the building. We gave out all the toys we had brought—and fortunately, we took plenty of toys. We played with the kids afterwards in a number of ring-around-the-rosy-type games and had a great time.

The mayor was gracious to our team and grateful for our presence. He had taken us out to dinner the night before and again for pastries and coffee once the toys had been passed out. He invited us to come back, promising to make things a little more orderly the next time. Tragically, a few weeks later the mayor was killed by a suicide bomber.

Chapter Ten

The Tyrant Is a Prisoner

"Ladies and gentlemen, we got him," Ambassador Paul Bremer announced. "The tyrant is a prisoner."

My cell phone lit up with one call after another as people near and far called to share their excitement in hearing the news of Saddam Hussein's capture. Iraqi friends and associates were calling throughout the day to express their appreciation for what the United States had done for them. Most Iraqis never imagined that such a day would come in their lifetime.

Passengers on buses and trucks leaned out their windows and shouted ecstatically: "They got him! They got Saddam!" Radio stations in Baghdad blared the news with celebratory music. Many residents fired small arms into the air in jubilation.

Iraqis could not believe the photos they saw in the morning paper. It was Saddam Hussein—their former president, ruler, dictator, and almost deified leader. He was considered super-human, magical and mystical, able to call upon the evil spirits from the other side; he was Master of the Red Genie Tribe. There he was—dirty, unshaven, with matted-down hair, crawling out of a rat hole—a grey-bearded homeless beggar.

"How could it be?" they asked out loud in amazement and disbelief. "How could it be like this?" Saddam, their strong and brave leader, surrendered without a shot being fired, not even a shot to end his own pathetic life. Where was the iron hand, the great military strategist, courageous commander, and brutal murderer of countless thousands?

Tracked down to his underground den, he was cornered like a rat. He was disheveled, powerless, and exhausted. He was suddenly demoted; he became a common man with no special powers that could whisk him away on a cloud of thunder or bring down lightening bolts upon his assailants.

The people of Iraq were rid of his tyranny forever. It was the end of the road for Saddam. He was now ready, as President Bush said, to "face the justice he denied to millions."

As I was tooling around the Green Zone in the Chief Wiggles Toy Bus, I saw two little sisters, ages six and ten, walking into the zone through one of the gates. I had seen them selling candy in our parking lots on occasion, so I thought it would be a good idea to give them a ride.

They were both so cute and so serious about their work. Through my interpreter I learned that they went to school in the morning and sold their candy in the afternoon. Then these two little entrepreneurs let us in on their sales secret. They had a list of things to say in English and they knew just how to pull on our heartstrings to get us to buy. The oldest would say in her sweetest voice, "I have no money," while tilting her head to the side and staring up at American soldiers with her big brown eyes. Like most, I am a total sucker for kids like that.

I was pursuing a broadening investigation involving the head of the police department that began following our successful counterfeiting raid. I had also been working with the Ministry of Justice, Ministry of the Interior, Internal Affairs, and a variety of other departments in a combined effort to take out some really bad apples from the bunch the Coalition had handpicked for key governmental positions in the new Iraq. Unfortunately, some of those individuals had been fraudulent in how they presented themselves to the Coalition; several lied about their rank and position prior to the war and the depth of their involvement with Saddam. Many of them fabricated stories about how they suffered greatly at the hands of their leader. Alarmingly, a few of these individuals had become quite powerful in a short period of time. Some of them were like little Saddams in the making, following in the footsteps of their recently ousted leader.

For the most part, the files on these crooks were in my hands. Several inside sources put proof behind the allegations regarding their corruption. We knew these people were bad, but we needed additional evidence to make it stick, hoping we had enough to remove them from office.

For the most part, my case was built around reports from citizens victimized by those abusive leaders. The citizens had firsthand knowledge of the injustices being committed and were making serious allegations against the individuals in question about their conduct before, during, and after the war. So many citizens and policemen had come forward with personal incidents and corroborating stories about these specific individuals, that it was difficult to not believe them. The files were getting thicker and the cases were getting stronger.

A team of CNN reporters was scheduled to travel with us on a trip to "Share Joys with Toys." I grabbed a quick bite to eat, knowing I would need the energy later on. I jumped in the bus for a quick jaunt over to the warehouse to load up the toys for the day's activities. We

Dr. Eaman (left) *was instrumental in arranging some of the deliveries of toys to hospitals.*

planned to go to an unfinished mosque where about 40 homeless families had settled in. We planned to spend a couple of hours with the children.

With the bus half-full of toys, the team was ready in the parking lot—Ali, Karim, Nabil, Renda, the CNN crew, and Dr. Eaman, who was going to show us the way. I did the usual briefing as far as the order of vehicles and where we were going. Then off we went.

We made our way through the back streets of Baghdad, our four vehicles clinging to each other as if hooked together like cars of a train, making every effort not to allow another vehicle to slide in between our caravan. Even though it was hard to lose sight of a bus, we didn't want to take any chances. We had heard plenty of stories how the bad guys would try to break into convoys to single out a vehicle for attack.

The great thing about driving in Iraq was the absence of traffic laws—at least it seemed that way. Every driver had to fend for himself—it was total vehicular anarchy. Yet it was amazing how well the whole system worked with no traffic lights, no lanes, no rules or regulations, and no one to enforce them if there were any. Anything was legal out on the road; you could drive anywhere and any way you wanted. It was "survival of the biggest," so the bus fared quite well. As long as the nose of your vehicle was ahead of the cars around you, you were in charge. The front seat passenger directed traffic from inside the car with synchronized hand gestures. Our loaded automatic weapons held tightly on our laps, just in case, gave fresh meaning to the term "riding shotgun."

It was a strange feeling to always have a 9mm pistol or an MP5 slung over one shoulder wherever I went, whether visiting a friend or buying ice cream or pizza. We had to always assume the worst was going to happen. Our motto was, "Locked and loaded, with a round in the chamber."

The unfinished Grand Mosque had become home to numerous families who had been evicted from their homes or apartments due to lack of money to pay for rent. Some families lived inside the unfinished structure and many more lived in cinder-block shacks and shanties around the perimeter.

One man, the head of his neighborhood block, stepped forward to help organize the activity. He wrote down the name of each family so as not to forget anyone and to make for an orderly distribution of our bounty. We came loaded with a thousand dollars worth of blankets and heaters, donated by the British owner of a clothing store, and of course, plenty of toys.

As we pulled up, a large crowd started to form, aware of our intentions and anticipating the free handouts. I exited my bus and quickly began shaking hands while offering the customary greetings of the morning. I made sure to extend my hand and offer up a smile to every man in the area. The women were all clustered together in their own group next to the men, in their long black burkhas, which covered all but their faces. Knowing their customs I wasn't going to shake the women's hands; but not wanting to offend, I offered up a cheerful "Good morning." The children were cautiously hiding behind the legs of the adults, not sure what to think about the arrival of the Americans. But as expected, they warmed up to us right away.

Maintaining an orderly distribution to every family was often a challenge, so we instructed them all to return to their homes and wait for us to come to them. One by one, with all of us toting imported blankets and kerosene heaters, we visited each home, speaking with the father, the mother, and many of the children.

The families were extremely poor, evidenced by their ragged clothes, worn out shoes, dirty appearance, and unsanitary living conditions. The kids were lacking in many things, most running around barefoot and with very little clothing on what was a chilly day. The flies seemed to be the only thing thriving in this area. The families lived in one-room mud huts without utilities such as electricity and running water.

As our team of givers went from house to house, several things about these families really impressed me. They were humble, gracious, and patient, and they were not ashamed of how they were living. They offered us tea, with several even asking us to stay for lunch. In contrast to all of the other toy drops, things went very orderly, with no one trying to get more than someone else.

After the parents received the blankets and heaters, we separated the kids into two groups, boys and girls. While the children were dancing round and round singing songs, I was in the middle handing toys to each child. We gave out stuffed animals, toy cars, and many other things. The children were all well-behaved, with no pushing and shoving to get the best toys.

Between locations, we stopped for a bite of flatbread and hummus. The tasty flatbread that is served and eaten everywhere is baked in a cone-shaped earthen oven. It sits upright with a fire inside on the bottom and an opening on top. The vendor takes the shaped pieces of dough and slaps them hard against the walls of the brick oven where the bread cooks to perfection. I was amazed that the bread didn't fall off the sides of the oven into the fire.

From there we dashed off to a children's hospital to visit the oncology ward where the leukemia patients were. We had just enough toys and stuffed animals for each child to get a couple of items. I was so pleased that we could offer up a small token of love to those overlooked and suffering children.

It was difficult to witness what these children were going through. We were deeply affected by the courage of both the mothers and the children and stopped by each bed to chat with them where possible. It was painful to realize that many of these children would not live to see their next birthday. The toys made a real difference, bringing a smile to the youngest and most innocent victims of Saddam's horrifying regime.

A distraught family from the Kurdish lands up north contacted me about an urgent meeting. They wanted to speak with someone from the CPA immediately about a terrible injustice done to their son. I agreed to meet with them that evening for dinner at a relative's home.

After eating a fantastic Kurdish-style meal, the father began to relay the tale of what had happened to his son, Hoshar, who was being held in the notorious prison at Abu Ghraib. The son had previously been the owner of a small but successful telecommunications company that had been awarded a multi-million dollar post-war contract with a global telecommunications company for the cell phone business in the Kurdish regions.

A second company, which had also been vying for the contract, fabricated an elaborate and malicious lie involving contrived terrorist connections to discredit Hoshar. With falsified documents in hand, the owner of the second company presented his case to the American military, who believed the story, arrested Hoshar, and threw him into prison.

Months later, after many attempts to get their son freed, the family was telling me the story that had sent their son to prison and pleading for my assistance to secure his release. The emotion in their voice led me to feel they were probably telling the truth; still, I had my interrogator antenna fully extended looking for any inconsistencies in their tale.

At the conclusion of the evening, I politely asked them for references of well-known individuals in the area who could verify their story. If it were true, then this was a terrible miscarriage of justice and their son deserved to be discharged immediately. They named several prominent individuals, such as the mayor of the city they were from, who could verify some of the details as well as establish Hoshar's high moral character.

After contacting these individuals, it didn't take long to figure out the web of deception that had been spun to entrap their son, who seemed to be innocent of all charges. After making my determination, I quickly sent off a letter to the MI officer in charge of detainees at Abu Ghraib. I stated the details of the case, outlined my findings, and petitioned for his release given the new information in the case.

When I received an email from Hoshar's brother informing me of his release and return back home, I breathed a sigh of relief.

The four Saddam heads which once adorned the CPA palace were gone forever. Every vestige of Saddam's oppressive and corrupt rule was being systematically eliminated. Even Saddam's barber, who harassed his employees in the CPA salon and stole their tips, had been removed. All but a handful of the 52 bad guys whose faces adorned the Deck of Doom playing cards had been caught. A linguist who was getting kickbacks from contracts was fired. The security director for one of the ministries had been removed after allegations of corruption and receiving kickbacks. The CPA was being beautified and cleaned up, inside and out.

For the first time since the start of the war, people in the south were able to travel to the north or wherever they wanted. People could think and say what they wanted at any time and place they chose. Freedom was growing and spreading.

I liked the cool crispness of the Baghdad winter, with nights even becoming cold at times. The temperatures were invigorating, giving me even more energy to go about my daily tasks.

Unexpectedly, I was hit by the news that my father, who was then 84, had just been diagnosed with colon cancer, the doctor giving him only a few months to live. He had been remarkably healthy all of his life, but was now unable to eat and required intravenous feeding. He had been hospitalized for the past few days and was being moved to a care center where he was told he would spend the remaining days of his life.

A wiry, dark-haired, and spunky kid, my dad grew up on a cattle ranch in Idaho and learned the value of hard physical labor before he started school. When Pearl Harbor was attacked, he showed his commitment to God, country, and hard work by enlisting in the Air Force, where he distinguished himself in the Pacific Theater. On Okinawa, at the height of the conflict there, it was discovered that he was color blind, something that should have been found before he ever left the ground. As a result, he was delayed from flying with his normal flight team that day. Miraculously for him, he was not aboard when the plane he should have been on was shot down by the enemy and all aboard were killed. A deeply religious man, he saw that as a sign that he still had important work God wanted him to do. I guess one of those tasks was to raise a son named Paul. The impact of his example and teachings can be seen in everything I do, both the silly and the significant. I hoped the Lord would grant him one more miracle and allow me to get home in time.

With only two months left before returning home, my pace quickened and my focus sharpened. I endeavored to finish up everything I had started. I felt a sense of urgency, knowing my time was getting short and I had much left to accomplish. With only so much time in a day, I was trying to get more organized and directed, my daily to-do lists growing longer and longer. I had stopped exercising and doing any other expendable activity in order to finish up all the projects I had started. Sleep had even taken a back seat to work.

I had been wondering how there could be a gas shortage in Iraq, with the second largest oil reserves in the world. But the gas shortage was real. Lines of waiting cars snaked down the street as people waited for hours to get their share of precious fuel.

As I conducted interviews and wrote up a report on the gas shortages, I learned that much of the allocated gasoline was being diverted to the black market. In many cases only one third of the allocation was actually being dropped off. Tanker trucks would pull into the gas stations and drive right through without dropping their load. The gas was then being sold on the black market in Iraq or was being exported to neighboring countries like Turkey and Iran, where they could receive three or four times the value. Much of the gas that was coming inbound from other countries, under government subsidies, was also being diverted to the international market to be sold at a higher price.

This national crisis was continuing as allegations surfaced that members of the Governing Council were personally benefiting from black market activity. The military began cracking down on the gasoline black market and was starting to see results.

All the major political parties in Iraq were jockeying for position, with many of them acting more like organized crime families. On the surface, most of them appeared to be helpful to Coalition forces, providing information to our various organizations and agencies regarding terrorists, Fedayeen, and other enemies. When you dug a little deeper, you found patterns of behavior that could destroy this fledgling democracy. I was relieved when we raided some of their offices, including those of the Iraqi National Congress.

Our earlier visit to the homeless families living around the mosque was prompted by Omar, a young boy who was concerned with the plight of the homeless children at his school. He told his mother of the need and she relayed the request to us. In recognition of his concern and efforts, we went to his school to make a presentation.

We pulled up to the school with a team of ambassadors of joy, toys in hand. It was strange, but understandable, to see several armed guards out in front of the elementary school. There had been several bomb threats at schools by individuals trying to disrupt and destabilize the situation. On one occasion, due to our intelligence, a bomb in a backpack at a school was discovered, removed, and diffused. The thought of a bomb going off in a crowded schoolyard made me shudder.

Stopping at the school office, we spent a few minutes speaking with the principal about the purpose for our visit. This middle-aged Iraqi woman, educated and devoted to her school children, was thrilled by our desire to recognize her student. I was impressed with her desire to offer an education for the homeless children when other schools had turned them away.

With the principal leading the way, we went to Omar's class-room with our team. It was a great moment for him as we presented a letter of appreciation from the CPA and several nice gifts made possible by donations from home. We gave him an artist's kit, with a full array of pencils, paints, markers, and a built-in easel. It was a specially selected item for Omar, a promising young artist.

As he stood in front of his class to receive the award, he just beamed, so eager to show his class what he had received. We took a class photo and encouraged the others to follow his example.

Many of my sources refused to be seen at the CPA palace for fear of being recognized by one of the Iraqi employees. As a result, I had been conducting more of my business at lunch and dinner meet-ings, both in and outside the Green Zone. There was one small cor-ner cafe within the Green Zone that was particularly conducive to those meetings, serving up a pretty tasty sampling of local cuisine and Iraqinized American food.

Since I was spending a good part of my day in this Green Zone cafe, the owner of the establishment assigned me a permanent park-ing space, with a hand-written sign that said, "Reserved for Chief Wiggles." I got to know all the employees quite well, often popping back into the kitchen to dance with the kitchen help to a song play-ing over the speakers. Everyone clapped while singing along to a popular Arabic tune with me. Spontaneous moments like those just increased my love for these people.

One evening after my meetings at the cafe, I was sitting out-side our hooch, waiting for my ride to pick me up. A car drove into our area with several Iraqis inside. As they pulled around to the front door, one of our interpreters dashed out to jump into their car, obviously being picked up to go somewhere. This was not a big deal, but I was alarmed by who I saw driving the car. The driver was the right-hand man of Chief Jamal of the police department, who we had been actively investigating since the counterfeiting bust.

Because of the nature of my business, I had enemies out there that would definitely take action against me if they could. If my enemies knew where I lived, once inside the Green Zone, they could really mess with me; I would be in serious jeopardy. This represented a major breech of security and potentially compromised my mission. From that day forward, I had clear reasons to be even more concerned about my safety.

My alarm went off at 5 AM on Christmas morning, indicating it was time for another one of our "Sharing Joys with Toys" excursions. Our two-day Christmas vacation allowed us the additional time we needed to take our toys to some previously untouched areas, including some areas up north.

We had the truck about half full when the mortars started coming in from just outside the Green Zone. I didn't hear any of them hit nearby, but felt it might be a good idea to take cover. All of us dashed into the basement of the adjoining building. With its tin roof and tin walls, our warehouse, even though guarded by tanks, would have been no match for any incoming projectiles.

We waited until the explosions stopped, which ended up being about an hour or so, before venturing back out. There was a lot of return fire from what sounded like Apache helicopters. Automatic weapon bursts were heard around the area, indicating that the insurgent thugs were on the run.

With the truck packed high with toys and clothes, we made a quick stop to meet up with Azad in another vehicle full of volunteers, anxious to participate in our toy delivery. We always traveled with at least two vehicles for safety and security reasons. With at least two fully loaded automatic weapons per vehicle, we departed. There was an unmistakable paradox as we departed to deliver toys to children, all equipped with AK-47s, MP5s, and various other weapons. I was personally armed with a pistol and an MP5 for my protection. If you hadn't seen the toys, you might have thought we were going out on a raid.

We traveled for several hours, making our way up north into Kurdish territory near the border with Turkey. Once we arrived in the town of Duhok, we picked up an Iraqi pediatrician who was anxious to guide us to our destination. In addition to his pediatric practice, he focused special attention on the psychological issues of children being raised in such difficult circumstances.

Leaving the paved highway, we made our way up a dirt road past a large open market. We pulled up to what appeared to be an old prison on top of a small hill. As if entering a large castle, we drove through an opening into the spacious open courtyard in the center of the building.

The doctor referred to this as "the compound" and began to describe the history of the building. It had been used as a prison back in the late 1990s to incarcerate, torture, and kill hundreds of Kurdish people at the hands of Saddam's special military unit. As I glanced around, I could see that the courtyard was encircled by hundreds of small rooms, with no facilities or amenities—just dark gray walls surrounded by dirt.

The rooms were occupied by otherwise homeless people, many of whom had lost a loved one at this facility. That explained why so many of the women were without husbands. There were over 200 families with some 800 children living at this site of imprisonment, torture, and death.

At first glance I couldn't see many children, but no sooner had we entered the compound than children began to run out from every

Saddam's prison in this Kurdish village was converted to living quarters for local families.

door and alley. Within minutes we were surrounded by squealing and laughing children as they began to figure out the purpose of our visit.

After meeting with the compound mayor, we decided to have all the children return to their homes, so we could visit with them one by one. It sounded like a good idea, but in actuality the children were too excited to stay inside patiently awaiting our arrival at their doorstep. Even so, we enforced the instruction by telling them to all return to their homes.

With a small group of men carrying our boxes, we proceeded to the first room in one corner of the building. Over the next five hours we went from room to room, handing out toys to every family. There were families in every nook and cranny, holed up in every corridor and usable area. There were even families on the roof of the building in makeshift homes, built out of sheets of wood, paneling or metal.

Conditions for those people were sparse. There were shared bathrooms and shared kitchens in some areas, while others had built in a gas stove to have their own kitchen. Most were without doors and the opening to each home was covered with a blanket or a tarp. Old worn out blankets or pieces of carpeting covered the cold cement floors of each home.

I quickly visited with the mothers of those beautiful children. There were no toys to be seen in any of the homes—no dolls, no toy trucks, no stuffed animals. The rooms were bare—only a few homes had furniture, a television or any appliances. There were no closets or bedrooms, just one room for the entire family and in some cases there were as many as ten people living in one room.

The mothers would line their children up in their simply appointed homes as I handed a carefully selected toy to each one. The children were so delighted to receive such an unexpected gift,

These Kurdish children were dressed in their finest for the morning of the toy delivery.

they would jump up and down while holding it tightly to their chest. Their eyes lit up and happiness filled the room.

As we entered some homes the mothers could be seen putting on their young daughters' finest little dresses as they prepared for our arrival. They really wanted to make a good impression on us; they greeted us with dignity, not embarrassment.

Children crowded in behind us as we walked from one home to the next. Some kids, hoping to get another toy, would sneak in line with the kids from another family; but I was too quick catching them in their act of deception. It was all done in good fun and laughter.

There were several little girls who would fight through the crowd of kids to hold my hand while I walked along, each time grabbing my hand again after exiting a home. They grabbed on to my clothes and my legs as I moved around the complex.

On many occasions the families begged me to stay for lunch or tea, hoping I would linger. But with so many families and so many children, we moved along as fast as we could, hoping to finish before it started to rain. But the rain came, bringing an end to a marvelous day full of both happiness and sorrow. Tired and wet, we left the compound well rewarded.

Back in my CPA palace office, sitting behind the Mother of All Desks, it was easy to become somewhat insulated from the gruesome realities of war. Hearing the concussion of an exploding bomb is not the same as seeing someone bleeding from a bomb blast. Seeing the strafing on a building from rapid arms fire is not the same as tending to those wounded by gunfire. Reading a body count report is not the same thing as seeing a dead body. I knew that my insulation left me with a somewhat distorted view of the war. Never once did I fire my weapon, but every time I pulled it to my shoulder, I knew I could be responsible for ending someone's life.

Our trip to Duhok shoved the reality of death right into my line of sight. As I was driving along the highway leading back to Baghdad, I cast my eyes to the side of the road and saw a dead Iraqi man lying in the ditch. His body was twisted and sprawled as if he had just been tossed out the door of a moving car. He was bloated and swollen beyond description. The smell stung my eyes and my throat. I gasped for air as I felt waves of nausea hit me like a Mack truck.

I suspect that this unknown man was a victim of Iraq's internal struggle. This poor fellow was probably involved in the black market—a readily available income source for Iraqis—and made a poor decision that had riled organized crime leaders. But it was still unsettling to come face to face with such an irreverent and brutal death.

Death is the vicious unseen partner in every war strategy. It reminded me of why we wanted this struggle settled once and for all.

Chapter Eleven

To Victory

"Chief, you've got 48 hours to remove yourself from the CPA."

That was all the notice I received that my mission was over. The call came from a colonel working under General Fast. The colonel told me to pack up my stuff and move myself to Camp Victory, not far from Baghdad International Airport (BIAP). He instructed me not to talk to anyone. I was to have no contact with anyone outside of my immediate team members.

I asked him what this was all about. It was abrupt. It was mysterious. It was unnerving. I tried to get any bit of information about why this was happening and why I couldn't have more time. He made it clear that he had called to give orders, not answers. I was assured someone at Camp Victory would be talking to me.

I was in shock after such an unexpected phone call. I didn't know where to begin. I didn't know how to end. Thoughts of all my unfinished work whirred through my head, as I tried to pull myself together. After making several attempts to delay my sudden departure, I complied with my orders to leave the palace.

The next two days passed like a desert sandstorm, propelling me into a whole new experience, one for which I was unprepared. I was deeply saddened to be hastily separated from the people I had grown to love, my fellow teammates, my interpreters, my colleagues at the CPA, and my dear Iraqi friends. As I made my rounds throughout the CPA and the Green Zone to say goodbye, there were many tender moments as I bid farewell to people I suspected I would never see again.

I had a hard time imagining life without my teammates. What would I do without them? What would they do without me? They were my lifeblood, my best friends. As I considered unfinished work, I was grateful to know there was someone in the office who could continue working on the case against Chief Jamal of the police department.

What about the work of Operation Give? Who was going to keep the work going? How were the toys going to get delivered?

It was extremely hard to part with Karim and Nabil, who had become such an integral part of our Operation Give team, Dr. Eaman, to whom I'd grown so close, and Renda, who had been with me every step of the way.

Chief Allen, along with two other teammates, Baghdaddy and Sergeant Charm, accompanied me to Camp Victory as a way to show their moral support for my predicament. With all of us loaded into the patrol vehicle, we drove away from the CPA palace, saying goodbye to my life in the heart of the new Iraq. As we drove away, I waved goodbye to my faithful Iraqi friends, Karim and Nabil, who were waiting in the parking lot. With tears in my eyes, I said a final farewell to Renda. It was a quiet drive from the CPA over to Camp Victory, a one-vehicle cortege. I had many thoughts racing through my head, all lapsing into uncertainty.

Camp Victory was on the southwest side of Baghdad, closer to the airport and inside the grounds of one of Saddam's other palaces. My teammates unloaded my gear at one of the tents so I could get settled in. As I watched my comrades drive off, there was a knot of unknowns twisting in my stomach. I had been kicked out of the kingdom, ostracized from the CPA palace that had been my home for the past six months, and dropped off without a word of instruction about what was going to happen. I was told only to report to the main office the next day.

In the morning I reported to the officer in charge of me. She just told me that someone would be in touch with me. Every day, for the next three weeks, I would walk up the dirt road from my tent to the main office. Each morning I asked the officer for an update on my situation. Each morning I began my long hours of waiting for someone who was supposed to talk to me. No one had an answer for me. The uncertainty was killing me.

Everyone else just went about their work as if I wasn't there. I had become a non-entity. With only a month remaining on my tour of duty, I found downtime frustrating. So little to do and so little time. It was as if aliens had snatched me up from my hectic, purposeful, and meaningful existence at the CPA, only to drop me off on an island full of people who were unable to see me or hear me.

Many acquaintances, former friends, and superior officers treated me as if I had leprosy, refusing at times to even acknowledge my presence when passing by. Preposterous rumors spread through the camp as others questioned my purgatorial existence, falsely suspecting me of selling illegal weapons and other such ludicrous explanations. All this time not a word was heard from any of those who were at one time my direct chain of command.

I spent my time over the next three weeks just sitting. There were no duties, no assignments, and no responsibilities. I looked forward to mealtime just to break up the monotony. The daily question and answer session was the same. "Is there someone here who can meet with me?"

"Not today."

I was alone except for my CPA team, who would show up every few days to check on my condition. Fortunately, there were also two captains from my home unit working at the same facility, who took me under their wing during this difficult time. But it was the unknown that was eating me alive—the stress of not knowing what this all meant.

The rest of my tentmates didn't return until around 10:30 PM, when their shift ended. It seemed odd to be in such quiet surroundings after having spent the last six months working late every night at the CPA palace with several of my close friends. I missed the rigor of the CPA, where late into the night people were still actively pursuing their daily activities.

The winter air was cold, forming puffs of vapor as I spoke. I felt unprepared for the briskness of the evening with my cold weather gear packed away in one of my three duffle bags. At night, not wanting to pull out my sleeping bag, I wrapped myself in a blanket and poncho liner. I resumed an acquaintance with my trusty old cot, after believing I had graduated from that lifestyle.

Occasional explosions broke up the silence of the evening as I sat alone at the far end of a tent, which was my new home. Within seconds the sound of sirens blaring could be heard in the distance. A few minutes later jets could be heard overhead, further securing the safety of our surroundings. The unmistakable sounds of war did nothing to diminish my heightened state of anxiety.

During this time of personal difficulty, there was a glimmer of peace about me, as I felt God letting me know that everything was going to work out and that this series of unwelcome events was all part of a larger plan. I spent much of my time reading, pondering, and reconnecting with my spiritual self, tapping into the heavenly powers which had accompanied me during other challenging times in my life.

Finally, I heard through my teammates that an investigative officer had been assigned to my case and he had questioned them about my conduct, my letter writing activities, and my involvement with the toy drive. Apparently, the letter I had written about Chief Jamal of the police department upset a few people back in Washington. In my letter I made no specific accusations about the Chief, but I did suggest that his record and behavior deserved further scrutiny.

Finally, some information about my case started emerging. I learned I would be staying at Camp Victory for as long as it took for the military to finish the investigation, then off for a short stay in Kuwait as a stepping stone on my journey home.

February 7, 2004, marked my one-year anniversary of being gone from home, mobilized for Operation Iraqi Freedom. My days were now slowing down to a virtual standstill. As I continued to wait for the outcome of the investigation, new replacements arrived from the States and the majority of my group prepared for their journey home. It was distressing to watch these comings and goings as I languished in military limbo. The Army had given me no indication whether or not I would be joining my group for the return trip home. I was stranded in some kind of suspended animation until such time as they decided what to do with me. Strangely, I was at peace, even while living in an area where background noises consisted of frequent bursts of automatic weapon fire and loud explosions.

Except for the bare essentials, my gear was packed and ready to go as I entered the last phase of my deployment. If all went well with the investigation, I expected to return with the rest of my original National Guard unit, but that was yet to be determined.

My pals from the CPA continued to come by every few days to update me on what they had heard about my case. Most of the time they didn't have much new information, but I appreciated their short visits and continual words of encouragement. Each of them gave me their take on what was going on after they were questioned by the investigative officer. They informed me on the line of questioning, which revealed for the first time why I was being investigated.

It appeared that the military was concerned about the letter I wrote to the Governing Council and my work with Operation Give. My buddies told me they had just learned it was against Army regulations for a serviceman to solicit donations. I swallowed hard as we said our goodbyes.

After they left, I was alone—really alone—and the isolation was taking its toll. As I pondered my uncertain situation, it suddenly occurred to me that I might be in deeper trouble than I had thought. What I had previously assumed was just a minor infraction had become something much more serious. Had my desire to bless Iraqi children tarnished my military service? Had my insistence on investigating corruption jeopardized my future? Had I put my family at risk? Was the full weight of the military justice system going to come crashing down on my head? My heart was pounding, my palms were sweating, and sleep was impossible. This was more stressful than incoming Scuds on the first night of the war.

To some degree, the wait was over. After interviewing all those associated or acquainted with me in any way, the investigative officer, Lieutenant Colonel Jones, finally made his way to Camp Victory to lay things out for me. Now into my third week of waiting, I was able to question him about what was going on. He was appalled to learn that I had been waiting so long without contact from anyone in my chain of command. He agreed that it was troubling that so many military comrades had distanced themselves from me like rats leaving a sinking ship. He was also bothered by the fact that no one had told me what the issues were.

Lieutenant Colonel Jones was preparing to return home upon completion of this investigative assignment. Thankfully, we both had the same goal—finish the investigation and leave Iraq as soon as possible. He was kind enough to lay out the plan for the next couple of weeks, schedule a time to question me, and inform me what the procedure would be. He seemed highly professional, one who would handle my case with fairness and integrity.

Lieutenant Colonel Jones' questioning lasted several days and covered every imaginable aspect of my work, contacts, and activities. He didn't badger me, but he was excruciatingly thorough. He was clearly after something. I was nervous, afraid, uncertain of the outcome, and unsure of the ramifications. The tables had turned. The interrogator was being interrogated. My days were filled with plenty of things to pray about.

It was apparent from his line of questioning that the military was uneasy about the time I spent on Operation Give. Was it interfering with my work? Whose vehicle was I using to make these toy drops? Whose computer was I using? It seemed that they were searching for anything they could use against me. I was beginning to feel that I had crossed some invisible line.

I was summoned to a meeting to review what had been determined in my case up to this point. I was seated on a chair across the room, while Lieutenant Colonel Jones was going over his findings with the Judge Advocate General (JAG) attorneys. They were just far enough away that I couldn't make out what they were saying. Periodically, Lieutenant Colonel Jones would approach me for a clarification and then rejoin the JAGs. They finally reached a stage where I could be included. The discussion was formal, somber, and rather threatening. Their faces made it clear that things were looking pretty bleak. They walked me through various scenarios, none of them pleasant. This appeared to be the beginning of a fairly lengthy process and no one seemed optimistic about the outcome.

Suddenly, a messenger entered the room to relay a message. Once granted permission to speak, he said, "I have a message for Chief

Paul Holton." I was already in hot water, I couldn't help but wonder how much deeper.

The attorneys pointed to me. The messenger turned and proceeded to tell me, "Call your commander back in Salt Lake City at once. President Bush is trying to get in touch with you. The President wants to have breakfast with you at the White House." I'm sure that everyone heard me almost choke.

"Stop everything," the JAG attorney said as he closed the file and stowed his legal briefs.

The tone of the meeting and the direction of the investigation had just been turned on its head. If the Commander in Chief was going to recognize my efforts with Operation Give, military attorneys weren't about to stand in the way.

I called home at once and after speaking with both my commander and my wife, I was instructed to call President Bush's senior speech writer on the White House staff immediately. The message originally delivered wasn't completely accurate. The President actually just wanted to applaud my efforts in getting toys to Iraqi children and needed my permission to quote from my journal and discuss what I was doing.

I phoned the White House immediately to inquire about the nature of their interest. "The President is giving a speech during the annual National Prayer Breakfast on Thursday and would like to discuss certain details about Chief Wiggles and the toys," the President's speech writer advised me.

"Of course, that would be great," I responded. I felt honored to receive that kind of recognition from my Commander in Chief. Frankly, I was surprised that knowledge of Operation Give had reached the White House.

With the speech writer on the phone, I confirmed details about the success of Operation Give and granted permission to use a quote from my Chief Wiggles blog.

As I walked back along the dirt road towards my tent, I rejoiced at the miraculous event which had just taken place. I found a secluded area, free from others walking by, and knelt in prayer. As I considered this miracle, I found myself overcome with gratitude. Tears streamed down my cheeks as I tried to grasp the meaning of it all. The President of the United States was going to applaud my efforts with Operation Give.

Lieutenant Colonel Jones submitted his report to his superior officers with the President's remarks positioned on the top of his findings. He was confident that the presidential commendation would turn the tide for me and would ultimately result in a favorable outcome. What a turn-around. I felt as though I could have flown home without a jet.

With almost all of my tentmates packed up and on their way to Kuwait, the tents at Camp Victory virtually empty, I was transferred to the military base at BIAP. It was like any other U.S. military base, with almost no evidence I was still in Iraq.

It was great seeing Major Price for the first time in six months. We embraced in a big manly bear hug as we saw each other again. There were only three of us left in Iraq, Major Price, Captain Hult, and me. The rest of the group had already made its way to Camp Doha near Kuwait City and was waiting for us to join them. We would be at Camp Doha for a couple of weeks, then off to Fort Carson for a week or so, and if all went well, back on home turf by the first part of March.

The two officers had each decided to stick around until I was given the green light to leave, even though they were both chomping at the bit to get out of town. It was reassuring to know I had friends who would stick by me when needed. But, with no end in sight to the waiting game, they were each beginning to wonder if, at some point, they would have to leave without me.

At BIAP the showers were hot and the porta-potties were clean. Add to this a fully equipped morale, welfare, and recreation (MWR) room with loads of movies, and it made this holding pen almost enjoyable. To top it off, Major Price and I had a room with a heater and a vehicle to share.

Then came the unexpected news that finally got me on my way. My wife called to inform me that my father's colon cancer was in its final stages with doctors giving him only weeks to live. Not knowing how long the Army was going to take to make a final decision, I told my wife to arrange a Red Cross message calling me home. After much diligence on her part, she finally got someone at the Red Cross to issue the request.

The Red Cross message arrived, requesting the Army release me to care for my dying father. Within a few hours the arrangements were made for me to return to the States for an undetermined period of time. Now the three of us were finally able to linkup with the rest of our men down at Camp Doha.

In anticipation of things to come, I awakened at 4:30 AM, Friday the 13th. In the crisp morning air, with a Humvee and a trailer loaded down with all our bags, we departed for the airport.

After sitting in the waiting room with hundreds of other home-bound soldiers, our flight was finally called up for its departure at 11:30 AM. We loaded up the C-130, sat inside its barren hull, facing each other in our webbed seats, for a quick hour-and-a-half flight down to Kuwait City. I was finally out of Iraq.

After unloading from the plane, I sat in the parking lot of the airport watching over our gear. I experienced a flashback of the thoughts and feelings I had a year ago when I arrived at that same airfield. For a moment, when I felt the sand-filled wind against my face and the noise of tents flapping in the wind, I thought it was beginning all over again.

I was snapped back to reality by hearing Major Price's voice. "How'd ya like a foot-long Subway sandwich?" Just knowing there was now a Subway franchise on base was all I needed to let me know that I had taken a giant step closer to home.

I was leaving, not arriving.

Chapter Twelve

Operation Give

As I walked into the bay of our group's living quarters at Camp Doha, each of the men in my home unit greeted me warmly. Outside of just a few individuals, I had not seen any of them since leaving Camp Bucca some six months earlier, and for many it had been the entire year.

We had all been greatly blessed and by the grace of God, we all made it back healthy and alive—not even a serious injury. It was a great reunion, filled with renewed love for each other. It was a group of men like no other.

One year earlier we were thrown to the winds, scattered all over Iraq. As I walked through the bay past their bunks, I greeted them, embraced them, high-fived them or patted them on the back. I was anxious to hear about their various escapades. Each had a remarkable story of great things they had accomplished.

Because of my dad's condition, I was only able to spend a couple of days at Camp Doha. I was taking an early emergency leave home to check on his condition, not wanting to experience another death in my immediate family in my absence. I stayed just long enough to out-process, making sure to turn in all the required equipment and take all of the necessary briefings, so that if at all possible, I wouldn't have to come back.

I am proud that I had the opportunity to serve my country in Iraq and to have participated in a great historical event—the toppling

Greeting my son and wife upon arrival in Salt Lake City.

of Saddam Hussein. I'm grateful I was able to serve the cause of freedom and to build and uplift the Iraqi people. I will always be grateful for my family who understood and sustained my desire to fulfill this mission.

Our homecoming was everything a soldier could hope for. As our C-135s touched down in Salt Lake City, joy washed over me like a tidal wave as I looked out the only window in the plane to see the hundreds of people inside the National Guard hanger holding banners and screaming as we touched down.

As I walked down the tarmac toward the cheering crowd, a small group of people holding a poster and a flag came running in my direction screaming, "Wiggles! Wiggles!" My family and a few close friends had broken past the barriers and were running down the tarmac towards me. It was great to embrace my family, especially my son Michael, who had been serving in Russia for the past two years as a missionary for the Church of Jesus Christ of Latter-day Saints.

It was complete joy knowing I was home, back among loved ones and back on American soil. I also realized that readjusting to life at home would take some time as the past year had been such a life-altering period.

Once home, I sat in my kitchen gazing out through a fog-framed window watching giant snowflakes fall aimlessly, bending pine boughs, and leaving the neighborhood swathed in a foot of

Among those greeting our arrival were (left to right) *U.S. Senator Orrin Hatch; Utah Governor Olene Walker; my wife, Keeyeon; U.S. Senator Bob Bennett; my son Michael; and cousin Steve Shepherd.*

white powder. The empty dog cage was covered with snow, causing me to reflect back on a time gone by when my dog, Jasmine, was still alive. I remembered playful times when we used to run around the yard together. I missed the past, was grateful for the present, and had great aspirations for the future.

The joy of being home was short lived when, after only four days, I received a call informing me that I would be returning to Iraq immediately in order to take care of a few remaining issues relating to my investigation. The Army had not yet decided what they wanted to do with me, but requested me to be present in Baghdad in order to make a decision. They expected me to be in Baghdad for about a month. I was not angry about going back to Iraq. Of course, I had no choice. But I also knew that the course of my life was in the Master's hands.

With the sound of the airplane engines gently humming in the background, lulling the passengers to sleep, I sat restlessly in my airplane seat trying to sort my mixed emotions as I returned to Baghdad. I was the only one returning to Iraq, so this trip would be very different from the last one, but perhaps just as rewarding. I was promised it would be short, but not necessarily sweet.

My transatlantic flight took me to Amsterdam for an onward flight to Kuwait City. About 30 minutes after leaving Atlanta, just after jutting out over the Atlantic, one of the flight attendants came down the aisle with a faxed message from Colonel Long. What now? Could it get any more tense? His short message shook me to the core.

"Chief Holton: There has been a change in your mission. Do not proceed to Kuwait. Get off in Amsterdam. Return and go home."

What possibly could have happened to bring about this sudden change of events? Officers in my direct chain of command and General Tarbet, the two-star Adjutant General for the Utah National Guard, had all been working tirelessly to influence a decision before

I was forced to return to Iraq. Ultimately, it was determined that the decision had to be made by the new U.S. Army General in Iraq. The Army concluded that a decision could be made without my being in Iraq. So it was paradoxical that the message came when I was 32,000 feet over the Atlantic.

A conclusion was made to have me attached to my unit in Salt Lake City until they determined if I was needed back in theater. This was music to my ears and an answer to many prayers. After several weeks of waiting and fretting over all the issues, the Army determined that I had committed no serious violation or crime. They issued a letter of admonishment instructing me to not write that kind of inflammatory letter again.

But the miracles didn't stop there. Once I returned home, my father went in for surgery for his colon cancer. After cutting out a piece of my father's colon, the doctors could find no other cancer in his system, after previously determining that it had spread throughout his body. Once hovering near death, he gradually improved and is back working in the garden and giving service in the community.

What began as a simple gesture, sharing a toy with a child in Iraq, has grown to touch the lives of millions. President Bush recognized this effort in his remarks at the 52nd Annual National Prayer Breakfast in Washington D.C. on February 5, 2004:

> Our people in uniform understand the high calling they have answered because they see the nation and the lives they are changing. A guardsman from Utah named Paul Holton has described seeing an Iraqi girl crying and decided then and there to help that child and others like her. By enlisting aid through the Internet, Chief Warrant Officer Holton

had arranged the shipment of more than 1,600 aid packages from overseas. Here's how this man defines his own mission: "It is part of our heritage that the benefits of being free, enjoyed by all Americans, were set up by God, intended for all people. Bondage is not of God, and it is not right that any man should be in bondage at any time, in any way." Everyone in this room can say amen to that.

There's another part of our heritage we are showing in Iraq, and that is the great American tradition of religious tolerance. The Iraqi people are mostly Muslims, and we respect the faith they practice. Our troops in Iraq have helped to refurbish mosques, have treated Muslim clerics with deference, and are mindful of Islam's holy days. Some of our troops are Muslims themselves, because America welcomes

Toys continue to pour in. These were collected by children at an elementary school.

people of every faith. Christians and Jews and Muslims have too often been divided by old suspicions, but we are called to act as what we are—the sons and daughters of Abraham.

Our work in a troubled part of the world goes on, and what we have begun, we will finish. In the years of challenge, our country will remain strong, and strong of heart. And as we meet whatever test might come, let us never be too proud to acknowledge our dependence on Providence and to take our cares to God.

The President's remarks and other reports fueled a groundswell of public support for Operation Give. This outpouring of donations has enabled Operation Give to grow and expand its work, not only to the children of Iraq, but to others facing critical needs such as the victims of the December 2004 tsunami in Southeast Asia. The need is great. The work goes on. And the generosity of the American people is boundless.

At a post-deployment gathering of my National Guard Unit, I overheard a fellow soldier make a few comments challenging the ethical and moral foundation of the War in Iraq. Of course, this was a hot button for me. So when the opportunity arose, I pulled him aside to discuss the issues he brought up.

As he shared his thoughts, I felt his sincerity but I could see he had been misled by the media as I heard him recite the familiar anti-war talking points. As a fellow veteran of Operation Iraqi Freedom, I thought he would have had a more accurate view of what we had contributed there. After we chatted a little longer, I got a better picture of how this happened. Although he had been in Iraq, he had never actually interacted with any Iraqi citizens and so he had no personal knowledge of their attitude about the war or the American presence there. He had spent the entire year inside the secure confines of a military base with a totally controlled environment. For all he knew, he might have been in Kansas, Cuba, or Kosovo. He had no firsthand knowledge of the very people he had come to liberate. I don't mention this to discount his sacrifice, but simply to point out that the experiences he and I had were so different that one might wonder if we had served in the same war.

He mentioned his frustration that we never found any weapons of mass destruction. Saddam Hussein, certainly had the capacity, the desire, and the history that led us to believe he had them. And they still may be there, concealed in one of his secret hideaways. After mass graves containing the bodies of over 300,000 men, women, and children were discovered, it could easily be argued that Saddam himself was a WMD.

He was also concerned about the findings of the Senate hearings that did not establish any direct connection between Saddam and the terrorist attacks of September 11, 2001, ignoring all the indicators and signs that established Saddam's long-standing relationship to terrorism. He terrorized his own citizens, he terrorized his neighbors, he terrorized his enemies and he terrorized his own family. The UN was afraid of him. Seventeen resolutions without action showed that.

From my point of view, it seemed that our involvement did not hinge on whether or not we uncovered Saddam's buried WMDs. Finding WMDs wasn't the focus of Operation Iraqi Freedom. Our success or failure in Operation Iraqi Freedom, as the name suggests, was about securing Iraqi freedom. That's what we were really fighting for. Freedom for that oppressed nation would lead to stabilizing a volatile and dangerous region of the world.

I remain convinced that this was about the Iraqi people and a chance for them to be free from the controlling grasp of Saddam Hussein. We had given the Iraqis high hopes in times past as we appeared to come to their rescue, only to pull away when international opinion forced us to abandon our plans. We stood by while

Saddam murdered thousands of Iraqis and Kurdish people who had risen up, showing their defiance, only to be squashed by this brutal tyrant.

I am not ashamed to say that, to a certain extent, it was also about oil. In this case the life blood of the world economy was being held hostage by a self-serving ruthless dictator, who continued to squander the nation's riches to suit his brutal penchant for murder, torture, and regional aggression. Our action was about bringing security, peace, and prosperity to a people and to an important part of the world. We saw the potential of bringing jobs, income, and opportunities to the masses of the world family in the Middle East.

But these reasons do not fully explain what propelled me into the life-changing experiences I encountered serving in Iraq. I was motivated by a higher force—one which enlightened my mind and enhanced my abilities. I witnessed divine intervention on numerous occasions, bringing about a sequence of interconnected events that could not have happened by chance.

I saw results achieved in miraculous ways, ruling out the possibility of intervention by any other power or force. Hurdles were overcome, obstacles removed, paths were cleared, and more than anything else, people were changed by the power of God. Hearts were touched by a Christ-like love, with every generous offer of kindness and with every concerned act. Military people from all walks of life and from all parts of our country repeatedly stepped out of themselves to display love, empathy, and concern for the people of Iraq.

The overwhelming majority of the soldiers I worked with carried this mission in their hearts and performed this mission with unrelenting energy throughout their tours of duty. We knew we could free Iraqis from the chains of bondage, but we also needed to show them what to do with this freedom as responsible citizens. Our lives exemplified the benefits and the responsibilities of a democratic society.

By spending time in their homes, I experienced their culture, tasted their hospitality, and saw through their eyes. My glimpse into their souls revealed their fears, concerns, weaknesses, and desires for their children's future. They openly expressed their love for us as fellow brothers and sisters, with hope for a brighter future for Iraq without the crushing despotism of Saddam Hussein.

My path was always prepared before me, as an intertwined sequence of events preceded my arrival at any given station. The hand of the Almighty touched individuals' hearts, softened their souls, and opened their eyes, to the end that many things moved smoothly along to resolution, in a totally unexpected manner. Miracle after miracle occurred as I traveled around that country.

The success of this operation was not in any of our hands; we were only tools in the Master's hands to bring about His desired results. It was not our vision, but His, we were pursuing.

There was much outside of our line-of-sight as we moved forward into unknown areas. We knew we were imperfect, that our successes would outweigh our mistakes. Our desire was that as common men and women we could perform uncommon feats to bring about the long-term development of these people and this new nation.

There is a human face on the war in Iraq and I saw it every day. The humanity, warmth, and love of the Iraqi people were made evident to me time and time again.

While in Iraq, I found myself as I discovered a passion for helping the people of Iraq, who had been without freedom or opportunity for decades. The work is far from complete. I still have higher aspirations to do something of greater value and to make a difference any way I can.

We, as Americans and members of the human family, cannot sit idly by while we watch a society being overrun by men driven by selfish aspirations for power, wealth, and control. We must chose to take some initiative in stopping these forces, so that the children of the world have hope for a brighter tomorrow. We cannot ignore the problems of the day, assuming they will disappear before our children will have to deal with them. The children of the world are our future. The future lies in what they can see; but we must paint a picture of hope. Many active duty military have painted that picture with their own sweat and blood.

I was encouraged by the interest that some news media had in Chief Wiggles and Operation Give. Once they understood what we were trying to do, they were anxious to catch a quick interview with me and hear our story. Even more exciting was the outpouring of generosity from family, friends, and neighbors back home, who wanted to contribute to "Share Joys with Toys." This kindness grew and expanded beyond just family and friends as thousands of Americans previously unknown to me contributed their time and resources to the work of Operation Give.

With the ongoing work of Operation Give, I have begun the next phase of my journey. My current stage is only a temporary layover, not an end or an arrival. Both America and Iraq have a bright future. I look forward to contributing to that shared future and experiencing the joy that comes with being involved and engaged in an abundant life.

When I went to Iraq, I was committed to give my all. Give my strength—every ounce I could muster. Give my time—every waking hour. Give my talents—everything I had to give. I knew there was a chance I would even have to give my life. But as I returned to American soil, I looked back and realized I had given more than I thought I would. I had given my heart.

Operation Give One Year Later

After a steady stream of life-changing events in Iraq, I felt compelled, upon my return, to continue the work I had started with Operation Give. An outpouring of generosity has enabled our organization to grow, evolve, and achieve phenomenal results.

With the help of our partners and numerous volunteers, Operation Give has flourished. A large part of our success at Operation Give has been a direct result of the generosity, dependability, and professionalism of FedEx. There are children all over Iraq, Afghanistan, and Sri Lanka that are smiling today because FedEx was willing to assist in the prompt and safe shipment of toys and educational supplies. Gary Becker and Terry Demuyt were especially helpful and generous with their time and energy.

Bridgepoint Systems, who is donating warehouse space for Operation Give, has made it possible to expand and streamline our operations. We are more efficient than ever.

Operation Give has had significant assistance from Clorox, Forever Young International, JibJab, and other corporate sponsors, who have graciously provided us with resources in the form of monetary contributions, product donations, and promotional consideration.

But the bedrock of support for Operation Give has been thousands of individual donors and volunteers. It's been amazing to watch Americans everywhere spearhead their own grass-roots donation drives in church groups, Boy Scout troops, schools, and neighbor-hoods. Many more have simply visited us at **www.operationgive.org** to make a monetary donation. Even though the lifeblood of our organization is made up of volunteers, contributions are needed to fund continuing operational costs.

Dr. Eaman, an Iraqi physician, has served Operation Give both here and abroad. She has been instrumental in insuring that every-thing gets delivered to the appropriate location. She has been a great help and we are indebted to her.

As a result of the generosity of American citizens from coast to coast, thousands of neglected children in the global community have received the clear message: "Someone out there cares about you." They have received much needed school supplies, medical supplies, hygiene kits, shoes, clothes, and toys.

The work goes on and goodness will prevail. The needs are great and with the continued help of corporate sponsors and compassion-ate individuals, we will continue to accomplish great things.

At Operation Give, we believe in miracles. It was a miracle that Operation Give ever started. It was a miracle that it was allowed to continue. And now, with the continuing help of so many, Operation Give is making miracles happen in the lives of children all over the world.

About the Author

Paul Holton, better known as "Chief Wiggles," is the founder of Operation Give, a humanitarian organization that ships toys, medicine, and educational supplies to children in war-torn and devastated nations throughout the world.

Many became acquainted with Chief Wiggles through his detailed and inspiring wartime "blog" on the Internet. As a chief warrant officer in the Army National Guard with 34 years of service, he has served as an interrogator and a Korean linguist. He has been to South Korea more than 50 times, functioning as an interrogation team chief, interpreter, or debriefer of North Korean defectors.

Holton was sent to the Middle East in 1991 during Operation Desert Storm, where he interrogated dozens of Iraqis. *Saving Babylon* recounts his experiences in Iraq during Operation Iraqi Freedom, from the start of the war through the capture of Saddam Hussein.

Paul has worked for FedEx for the past 15 years, and is currently a world wide account manager. He has taught supply chain management and operation management at the University of Utah and at Brigham Young University. He is the father of four children and resides in Salt Lake City with his wife, Keeyeon.

Order Form

❑ Please send *Saving Babylon: The Heart of an Army Interrogator in Iraq* to the following address:

Name: _____

Address: _____

City: _____ State: _____ Zip: _____

Telephone: (_____) _____

Email: _____

Quantity: _____ x $19.95 = _____
Shipping (in U.S.): + $3.75
    (add $2.00 for each additional book) + _____
Add $1.25 sales tax per book for orders shipped to Utah + _____
Total: = _____

Payment:
❑ Check
❑ Credit Card:
    ❑ VISA   ❑ MasterCard   ❑ AMEX

    Card number: _____

    Name on card: _____

    Exp. Date: _____/_____

Send to:
    Saving Babylon
    P.O. Box 520055
    Salt Lake City, UT 84152-0055

For fastest service, order online at www.savingbabylon.com